The Art of Teaching Adults

THE ART OF
TEACHING ADULTS

Elinor Lenz

University Extension
University of California—Los Angeles

Holt, Rinehart and Winston

New York Chicago San Francisco Philadelphia
Montreal Toronto London Sydney
Tokyo Mexico City Rio de Janeiro Madrid

Library of Congress Cataloging in Publication Data

Lenz, Elinor.
  The art of teaching adults.

  Bibliography: p. 111
  Includes index.
  1. Adult education. I. Title.
LC5215.L45   374   81-13176
ISBN 0-03-054651-6   AACR2

CBS COLLEGE PUBLISHING
Holt, Rinehart and Winston
The Dryden Press
Saunders College Publishing

Education is an act of love and thus an act of courage. It cannot fear the analysis of reality or under pain of revealing itself as a farce, avoid creative discussion.

Paulo Freier
Education for a Critical Consciousness

Psychology is a science, while teaching is an art.

William James
Talks to Teachers on Psychology

CONTENTS

INTRODUCTION

This book is addressed to present and prospective teachers of adults and especially to the growing number of part-time teachers who are responding to the need for men and women to share their knowledge and experience with adult learners. Much of the material in the book should also be of interest to administrators of community colleges, four-year colleges, and universities and their continuing education divisions as well as to businesses, industrial firms, and government agencies that conduct educational programs for their employees. All these institutions and many others are involved in the pluralistic and infinitely diverse enterprise of adult education.

There has never been a better time for the teacher of adults than the present. Demographic trends indicate that we are fast becoming a society in which people in their middle and later years outnumber those under twenty-five. An upsurge of interest in adults is manifesting itself in any number of ways, from television, which, sensing a promising market, has begun presenting mature people in commercials, to institutions of higher education, which, threatened by declining enrollments of traditional-age students, are suddenly discovering an untapped source of replenishment in those beyond the traditional age.

Adult education has become the fastest-growing sector in American education. Adult students are being referred to as "the new majority." Current indications are that this trend will continue through the 1980s, aided and abetted by such social changes as the expanding movement of women into the work force; evolving attitudes toward the needs of minorities, the elderly, and the handicapped; and the need for retraining to meet the demands of new technologies.

These developments are moving adult education in directions that are breaking sharply with tradition. Within educational institutions, there has been an explosion of new formats, structures, methodologies, and delivery systems, among them courses given over radio and television, universities without walls, credit for "life experience," and a variety of external-degree programs. Experimentation and innovation are taking place in the larger community as well: in business, labor, the military, churches and synagogues, civic groups. Where all this growth and ferment are leading depends to a large extent upon the teachers of adults, who occupy a key role in this expanding universe of "lifelong learning."

Historically regarded as a second-class pursuit by the educational establishment, the teaching of adults is taking on new dimensions and acquiring enhanced status. While teachers of adults are gaining this long-delayed recognition, they are also facing new problems and challenges as they adapt to today's changing realities in adult education.

The primary purpose of this book is to help teachers of adults perform more effectively in this new learning environment. The book is an outgrowth of my work at UCLA Extension with both new and experienced teachers, and much of the material in it is based on their interaction with the adults they teach. Interviews with adult students, counselors, educational psychologists, and others who work with adults have yielded valuable insights. I have also dipped into the wealth of exciting recent research in adulthood and adult learning for information on techniques, strategies, and communication skills that are readily adaptable to the kinds of problems and situations teachers of adults commonly encounter.

An underlying assumption of the book, as suggested by the title, is that teaching adults is an art. But "art" in this sense does not refer to some mysterious intuitive gift or talent possessed by a favored few. Applied to the transaction of teaching adults, the definition is as stated by Webster, a "power" that can be acquired and that can therefore be regarded as a creative process with its own integrity and validity.

The creative teacher is one who can help learners revitalize their individual resources and enhance their capacity for growth and change. When the process is working effectively, there is a heightening of self-awareness in both teacher and learner that pushes back constraints and limits that may have been imposed by previous experience. It is through this mutuality, this sharing of consciousness and experience, that the teacher of adults can make a valuable contribution, not only to the individuals concerned but also to the community in which they live.

A Note on Terminology

Definitions of a few terms that appear throughout the book are offered for the sake of clarity:

In adult education, the term "learner" is preferred to "student," since "learner" connotes a more active role in the learning process. This usage accords with a basic distinction in adult education between "schooling" or "education" and "learning." In observing this usage, I have used the term "student" in a generalized sense, referring to a person who is enrolled in a program of study. "Learner" refers to a person who is actively involved in learning.

"Traditional" and "nontraditional" refer to either programs or students. In the case of programs, "traditional" describes the established mode, "nontraditional" any departure from this mode. "Traditional-age" students are those who have moved in an uninterrupted sequence from primary school to college graduation. (They may be several years older if they are graduate students.) Students of "nontraditional age" may be anywhere from the mid-twenties onward and in most cases have been out of school for some time before resuming their education.

The term "class" is associated with traditional schooling. For the purposes of this book, I have relied upon the definition provided by Snyder and Ulmer:"a collection of individuals who are somehow attracted to a common area of interest and study."*

---

*Robert E. Snyder and Curtis Ulmer, *Guide to Teaching Techniques for Adult Classes,* Prentice-Hall, Englewood Cliffs, N.J., 1972 p. 12.

Chapter 1

THE
TEACHING-LEARNING
CONNECTION

In traditional American education, the teacher has been assigned authority on the basis of the expertise that he or she brings to the task. Requirements for certification as a teacher have varied over the years and continue to vary geographically, but essentially, the teacher has been viewed as someone trained for the profession, pursuing it full time, and solely responsible for the education of the students in his or her charge. The student is perceived as a child or adolescent, someone in the formative stages, who is being prepared for the tasks and responsibilities of adult life. The relationship between the two is that of a giver and a receiver, the former an active agent, the latter a passive receptor.

From these roles and relationships flow a series of assumptions that have provided the substructure of American education: that teaching, or pedagogy, is an activity without a feedback loop, a transmission belt that goes one way, reaching at the other end an immature, unformed human being, namely, a student; that this activity takes place within fixed points of the student's life, normally between the ages of six and twenty-two; that it occurs at certain hours within buildings designed and set aside for the purpose; that both teacher and student are engaged full time in their respective tasks.

These assumptions are clearly inapplicable to adult education. As a teacher of adults, your dealings are with people whose ages extend from the twenties, and sometimes younger, to the seventies, and sometimes older, with the bulge in the thirty-five to fifty-year range. From these adult learners you can receive as much as you give and sometimes more. In order to do an effective job of teaching, you require constant feedback; communication flows two ways, and you are continu-

1

ally adapting and adjusting your teaching skills, plans, and objectives according to the information that comes back to you.

PROFILE OF THE ADULT LEARNER

Adult learners are people whose lives are overflowing with commitments, obligations, burdens of one sort or another. They have jobs or professions that occupy a substantial portion of their time, or domestic responsibilities, or, in many cases, both. The time and energy they invest in learning must compete with all the personal, social, family, community, and other tasks, responsibilities, and diversions that press upon the lives of most adults.

Among these learners, you may expect to find people like the following:

Women with new interests. These women include those with grown children (the "empty nest" syndrome), widows, divorcees, seeking psychological support to prop up their shaky sense of self at this difficult time. A questionnaire given to these "resuming women" by a New York college asked them to state their reasons for returning to school. They offered such responses as "I want to grow up and find my own identity," "I need constructive interests outside the home," "I'm feeling stagnant and want a meaningful career." Your students will also include women who want to upgrade their job skills or move in a new career direction.

Midlife career changers. These people are reacting against the traditional view of a career as a continuous and progressive pursuit of one occupation. In a highly advanced technological society, there is the ever-present threat of occupational obsolescence. Also, new ideas about work and the work ethic, about the "quality of working life," are encouraging people in midlife to move in new job directions in order to find greater satisfaction and fulfillment in their work. A government study on career education suggests that an emerging psychological and sociological definition of a career is "the sequence of positions occupied by a person during the course of a working and work-related life. This takes into account the fact that most people change occupations several times during their careers and that occupational mobility can be horizontal rather than vertical."

Retired people. These men and women enjoy mental activity and regard learning as a pleasurable way to fill their newfound leisure time. A UCLA study of people in their sixties and seventies which was conducted by their peers revealed a preference for noncredit offerings given in the daytime with an emphasis on current affairs, health, and the liberal arts.

Adult learners are people who are learning of their own free will. Except for mandatory continuing education for the professions, certain special court-ordered programs, and training programs funded by government and industry, adult education is largely voluntary and is paid for by the learners. These learners have experienced some of the pangs, joys, frustrations, satisfactions, anxieties, disappointments, resignations, and moments of exhilaration that make up adult life. They have come to you with certain hopes and expectations. What they hope to gain covers a broad range of interests, as indicated in Table 1.1 and Appendix A.

TABLE 1.1.   Adult Students' Choices of Subject Areas

PROBABLE MAJORS OF PART-TIME ADULT DEGREE-CREDIT STUDENTS, FALL 1978*		ADULT REGISTRATIONS IN NONCREDIT INSTRUC-TION, 1977—1978[†]	
Business	28%	Health professions	12.3%
Health professions	15%	Business and management	10.5%
Social sciences	9%	Fine and applied arts	9.5%
Education	7%	Physical education and avocational instruction	7.9%
Engineering	5%		
Fine arts	5%		

* Lewis C. Solomon, Joanne J. Gordon, and Nancy L. Ochsner, *The Characteristics and Needs of Adults in Post secondary Education* (Draft), Higher Education Research Institute, Los Angeles, October 12, 1979.

[†] Robert Calvert, Jr., "Survey of Noncredit Activities of Colleges and Universities for the Year Ending June 30, 1978" (Early Release), National Center for Education Statistics, U.S. Department of Health, Education, and Welfare, Washington, D.C., August 6, 1979.

Note: Excerpted from data; columns do not total 100%.

Source: Ronald H. Miller, "A Decade of Data on Adult Learners," *The College Board Review* 114, Winter 1979—1980, pp. 16, 17.

LEARNING LOCATIONS

Adult education may take place in a regular classroom in a community or four-year college or university, or it may take place in such locations as:

Basement of a church
Living room of a private home
Botanical gardens
Newspaper office
Radio broadcasting station
TV studio
Military base
Penal institution
Railroad train

Cruise ship
Restaurant
Historic site
Museum
Library
Hospital laboratory
Real estate office
Hotel
Theater
Artist's studio

Your classroom is actually the entire community. In the case of field study trips, every corner of the globe becomes a potential site for learning.

ROLE DIVERSITY

As a teacher of adults you may fill many different roles. In addition to classroom instructor, you may serve as a guest speaker in a lecture series, a moderator for a panel program or a panelist on the program, a mentor for a student pursuing independent study, a coordinator of a conference, a participant in an educational radio or TV program, or a course designer in an open-learning project.

In performing these roles, you may be employed by a high school adult education division, community college, university extension division, church, professional association, public agency, or private corporation, or you may be a self-employed entrepreneur designing and presenting educational programs in a variety of settings.

THE TWO TEACHING CATEGORIES

In adult education, teachers can be roughly classified as full-time and part-time. In the first category are those who have been trained as teachers and are fully credentialed—with either a B.A. degree and teaching certificate or an M.A., or, in the case of most college and university instructors, a Ph.D. These people regard teaching as a life career, and in most cases are or have been or hope to be employed as full-time teachers. The second group takes in those who have had little or no training in pedagogy and who are engaged in other occupations; teaching is, for them, a secondary career or a form of moon-lighting.

In the four-year colleges and universities, particularly the more prestigious institutions, credit courses in the extension divisions are taught either by full-time academics, often regular faculty employed by the particular institution, or by adjunct faculty. Extension divisions that offer academic degrees often require that the instructor be recruited from the regular faculty or at least have a Ph.D. in the subject to be taught.

Academic instructors bring to their adult students a depth of knowledge in the subject area. Trained in a discipline, they are attuned to research and scholarship and are primarily interested in advancing their specific area of study. College and university faculty are essentially specialists whose contribution is especially valuable to mature students seeking degrees or those who, for personal enrichment and stimulus, wish to obtain a scholarly grasp of the subject.

Part-time instructors have been flooding into adult education as a result of the growth of noncredit study and career education. These instructors, who in the overall picture greatly outnumber the full-time teachers, may or may not have academic degrees; some of the most successful among them have nothing beyond a high school diploma. Their value to their students consists of the practical experience they can offer. Who is better equipped to teach journalism than the working journalist, or cooking than the chef of a leading restaurant, or fund raising than the successful professional fund raiser? Here the emphasis is on learning a skill or acquiring useful information or both, and the instructor is expected to be able to relate the learner's needs to the real world in which the skill and information are to be applied rather than to some abstract conceptual scheme.

Part-time teachers frequently have the opportunity—in many cases, are required—to design their own courses, since these are usually new offerings. This may be done with the assistance of a program administrator on the staff of the institution offering the course. The teaching-learning connection plays an important part in the process when feedback from learners—through needs assessments, evaluations, and other sources—is incorporated in the design of the course. Procedures for designing new courses and programs vary from one institution to another, but generally the teacher has ample latitude for exercising originality in developing additions to the existing curriculum.

MOTIVATIONS

Whether a teacher is full-time or part-time, the financial rewards for teaching adults are, with few exceptions, moderate to low in a generally low-paying profession. For some campus faculty, teaching in extension programs offers a readily available way of supplementing their regular income. For people with part-time or freelance occupations, it can provide that extra financial margin that makes it possible for them to stay afloat financially. Money, though, certainly does not rank as a leading motivation for the teacher of adults. What is it, then, that attracts so many people to the field? As a teacher or would-be teacher of adults, what are your reasons for choosing this area of teaching?

Full-time teachers usually reply without hesitation, "Because I enjoy it." Compared with high school or college students, adults are a pleasure to teach: they are highly motivated, responsive, conscientious, and appreciative. It's what teaching should be and rarely is—a mutually stimulating, enriching experience.

Part-timers also put enjoyment at the top of their list of reasons. A corporate executive who teaches business communication says, "At the end of a hard day hassling with the problems of the job, it's a turn-on to meet with a group of people who respect you and think you have something to offer them." A survey of public relations instructors in a large university extension division yielded several variations on the following theme: "Considered going into college teaching at one time. Enjoy doing just that now on a part-time basis. Believe in the importance and value of professionals working in the field teaching others who are interested in the field. A practical 'how to' approach is of real service in preparing others for a career in public relations."[2]

A full-time professor of history at a private college gives her assortment of reasons as follows: "Teaching adults offers an opportunity to use a creative approach in putting together a course. . . . You get positive ego strokes from the experience—adolescents are inhibited about showing emotion or gratitude, whereas adults are free and open in expressing their appreciation."

Other motivations, especially among part-time instructors, include some that are clearly self-serving. There is the clinical psychologist who wishes to build up his private practice, the author promoting her book, the politician running for local office, the public relations consultant who sees the university connection as good public relations for himself, the realtor who hopes to pick up a couple of clients, the actor between jobs, teaching "speech for acting," who thinks the "exposure" will be beneficial. The relationship between such motivations and teaching performance will be examined in our discussion of ethical issues in Chapter 9.

Probably most teachers approach the task with a mixture of motives. In addition to those we have mentioned, they may find that an occasional stint of teaching offers them a psychological pickup, the "positive ego strokes" referred to by the academic instructor quoted above. Or they may feel the need to pass on to others their special area of expertise, a skill they have mastered, a leisure activity they have enjoyed. Whatever their reasons, most teachers of adults agree that it is a job worth doing and worth doing well and that the rewards, though often intangible, fully justify the investment of time and effort.

ATTRIBUTES OF AN EFFECTIVE TEACHER

In a field as open-ended and dynamic as adult education, is it possible to establish standards and criteria for effective teaching? The problem of instructional criteria in the teaching of adults has a long and checkered history. In the early days, when Ralph Waldo Emerson and Henry David Thoreau were delivering their Lyceum lectures and William Jennings Bryan was emblazoning the Chautauqua trail with his "Cross of Gold" speech, the most desirable characteristic for these popular educators was the ability to draw and hold an audience, or what we today would refer to as "charisma."

When adult education began taking on such urgent responsibilities as the Americanization of the immigrants, the ability to set off verbal fireworks became less important than the patient, plodding efforts of the dedicated teacher. The famous teacher of immigrants Henrietta Szold has been described as "quiet," "earnest," "absorbed in her work," "almost painfully intense."[3] In 1933, Hilda Smith, an educator prominent in the labor movement, suggested the following requisites for the teacher of adults:

Knowledge of the subject and ability to communicate it
Knowledge of teaching techniques
Willingness to learn from the students and relate teaching to their experience
Intellectual integrity
A broad cultural perspective free from prejudice
Interest in students as individuals and belief in their desire to learn
Warm, sympathetic personality
A sense of humor

It would be difficult today to improve upon Hilda Smith's criteria. Note the humanistic flavor of these criteria and the fact that she does not include formal degrees or credentials among the items on her list. The students she was concerned with were working people who saw education as a means of improving their economic position and helping them realize the American dream, but her criteria are appropriate for teachers of adults whatever the background or income level of their students.

The attributes of an effective teacher flow from the characterization of the teaching activity as an art, rather than a science or even, as some would have it, a business. Just as the artist must have a highly developed sense of the unique, so the teacher of adults must be sensitive to the individuality of each learner. It is highly unproductive to attempt to classify mature people as is often done with young students—below average, average, above average; or by grade—A students, B students, C students, and so on. This is a doubtful procedure with students of any age, but particularly so with adults, whose involvement with learning is too various and complex to lend itself to facile grouping and labeling.

Teachers who look upon what they are doing as an art are less likely to be bound by rules or precedents or lesson plans or immutable objectives. They are able to share with their students the experience of learning as fluid, life-enhancing, open-ended. They have an enthusiasm for their subject which is infectious, and, proceeding creatively rather than mechanically, they leave room for the unexpected and the unpredictable.

Unfortunately, many teachers of adults as well as in elementary through college levels regard what they do as something other than a creative activity. Some see it as a form of behavioral science governed by Skinnerian formulas of reinforcement and punishment, with the carrot and the stick as the principal tools. Others look upon it as a kind of business—the "information dissemination" business, as Postman and Weingarten phrased it in their book *Teaching as a Subversive Activity* (1969). According to this view, students are "products" of the process and are evaluated according to certain preset standards. The financial pressures and competitiveness of adult education have generated a "business mentality" that perceives the curriculum as educational "merchandise" to be attractively "packaged," with the students as "education consumers." In fact, the actual teaching and learning process has very little in common with either science or business. "We are dealing with human minds, not dead matter" is how Alfred North Whitehead defined the fundamental difference.[4]

The teacher of adults is, above all, a sensitive human being who recognizes that the primary purpose of education is to allow a person to come into full possession of his or her powers and who therefore places special emphasis on the teacher-learner relationship.

TEACHING-LEARNING MODELS

In adult education, the connection between teacher and learner is crucial, affecting every stage of the learning process. For this reason, the traditional model, which sets the teacher up as a kind of parental authority figure, acting unilaterally on behalf of the young, is clearly inappropriate. In recent years, models have been evolving which are more suitable for adult students and which represent a radical departure from the traditional paternalistic relationship. Three basic models are presented in Table 1.2.

There are several features the relationships in Table 1.2 have in common: the teacher-learning equation is in balance, with roughly equivalent obligations and responsibilities on both sides; compulsion is replaced by cooperation. Also, the teaching function becomes many-faceted: as "facilitator," "catalyst," "knowledge broker," "change agent," you are helping adults cope with such endemic contemporary problems as fragmentation, passivity, and adaptation to rapid change.

TABLE 1.2.   Teaching-Learning Models

RELATIONSHIP	CHARACTERISTICS	OUTCOMES
Host-guest	Host treats guests as peers. Makes every effort to create comfortable and relaxing environment.	A good host can expect guests to return in the future.
Client-consultant	Consultant must be able to assess needs, strengths, and weaknesses of clients. Consultant serves primarily as adviser, leaving responsibility for following advice to clients.	When expectations are met, clients are satisfied with services of consultant.
Partnership	Both make investment and both expect a return. Sharing and openness on both sides are required.	When both sides live up to responsibilities, partnership is usually successful.

LEARNING FROM LEARNERS

When there is a productive relationship between teachers and learners, the benefits that flow in both directions can take any number of forms. On the teacher's side, there are few other activities that can contribute so much to individual development and awareness. Adult learners offer a fascinating mix of ages, cultures, religious beliefs, political persuasions, income levels, education, and experience. There are teachers who claim to have learned more about human relationships from one or two terms of teaching adults than from any other experience in their lives. One teacher says, "It is difficult to hang on to your prejudices when you've taught adults for a while. I recommend it as a cure for bigotry."

Since adult learners often bring a high level of sophistication and professionalism to their studies, your dividends may assume more concrete forms. A freelance writer teaching a journalism class reports that a collaboration with one of his students on a series of articles led to publication in a national magazine. A historian specializing in the American West tells of a student research project that later proved helpful in her own research. The coordinator of a lecture series on local government who invited several public officials in the area to be guest speakers was offered a job on the staff of one of them. Examples like these can be multiplied many times. As you might expect, the more you bring to your teaching, the more you are likely to take away with you.

BACKGROUND AND TRAINING

In considering the teacher's background and preparation for the infinitely diverse field of adult education, it is helpful to begin with two broad classifications: generalist and specialist. Within the former are those who teach liberal arts, fine arts, and the social sciences; the latter group includes those in such professional fields as health sciences, law, engineering, architecture, and urban planning. Since continuing education for the professions requires a high degree of specialization and ongoing involvement with the latest developments in the field, instructors for professionals are often members of the professional areas in which they are teaching and may be actively engaged as practitioners in their respective fields.

In general, the most useful preparation for the teacher of adults is a thorough knowledge of the subject to be taught plus some practical experience. College and university faculty who have never ventured beyond the walls of academia, brilliant scholars though they may be, are often ineffective in teaching adults because of their unfamiliarity with the practical application of their disciplines. This problem is more likely to occur among faculty in the liberal arts than in the scientific and technical fields, since the scientists and technicians are frequently sought as consultants by government and industry, where they have an opportunity to apply their knowledge. In the liberal arts, the growing number of unemployed Ph.D.'s may serve as a valuable resource for the education of adults since many of these young scholars are being forced to take employment in nonacademic occupations.

Many excellent instructors have acquired their experience as volunteers in civic and community organizations, as members of the clergy, or as Peace Corps workers. These public service activities provide intensive experience in human relations and in communicating with diverse publics; therefore, they are a valuable training ground for teaching in adult education.

A question that frequently arises, particularly among part-time teachers, is, How important are courses in pedagogy? It is difficult to address this question without attaching a string of modifiers and qualifiers. Much depends on what and where you are planning to teach, how you relate to mature people as individuals and as a group, what your skills are in organizing and communicating information. There are certainly advantages to be had from courses in educational psychology and sociology, in the use of audiovisual equipment and materials, in teaching methods and communication skills. These tools of the trade can help give you, among other things, the poise and confidence that you may need, particularly if you are an inexperienced instructor. But your most important training will take place on the job, from your participation in the dynamic and open-ended process of adult education.

THE SPECIAL BOND

The teaching-learning connection in adult education is, in essence, a bond that is established through the give-and-take of ideas, information, skills, experience. It is a relationship that calls for active participation on both sides, and as in any other cooperative venture, the gains achieved are in proportion to what is invested by the participants. There is no easy formula for either teaching or learning, and becoming an effective teacher of adults is a gradual development. A good starting point, which precedes the mastery of teaching tools and strategies, is an understanding of how adults learn.

REFERENCES

1. Donald E. Super, Career Education and the Meaning of Work, U. S. Department of Health, Education, and Welfare, Washington, D.C., June 1976, Chap. II, p. 5.
2. UCLA Extension, *Survey of Public Relations Instructors,* 1979, p. 5.
3. Irving Howe, *World of Our Fathers,* Harcourt, Brace, Jovanovich, New York, 1976, p. 227.
4. Alfred North Whitehead, *The Aims of Education and Other Essays,* New American Library, New York, 1953.

Chapter 2

HOW ADULTS LEARN

One of the most complex and intriguing questions in educational psychology is, How do adults learn? For the teacher of adults, this question is as basic as the alphabet and it opens up such lines of inquiry as: Does learning take place differently in adults than in children? Are there certain conditions—physical and psychological—that affect adult learning? Do adults have special learning problems that impede their progress?

Investigators digging in the rich soil of adult learning have produced a bountiful harvest of theories and hypotheses. Much of the groundwork for current thinking on the subject has been laid by humanistic psychologists, such as Carl Rogers and Abraham Maslow, and by adult educators, among whom are Cyril O. Houle, Allen Tough, Malcolm Knowles, and Alan B. Knox. They and other researchers have been in the forefront of the shift that has been taking place since the 1970s, a development that Malcolm Knowles identifies as "the outgrowth of the 'humanistic question' for the complex dynamics of growth and development by unique individuals in interaction with their environments."[1]

Most theorists agree that learning, whether by adults or children, involves change. It is not enough simply to transmit information or ideas, if these remain inert and are received into the mind, as Alfred North Whitehead has said, "without being utilized or tested or thrown into fresh combinations."[2] Change through learning involves the acquisition of new knowledge, habits, or attitudes leading toward a better comprehension of the self and the social environment. Through this expanded understanding, the individual is better able to make both personal and social adjustments.

A recent report to the Club of Rome on learning in an age of scientific and technological advance defines learning as "an approach, both to knowledge and to life, that emphasizes human initiative. It encompasses the acquisition and practice of new methodologies, skills, attitudes and values necessary to live in a world of change. Learning is a process of learning to live with new situations."[3]

LEARNING AND EXPERIENCE

For adults, learning is closely associated with experience. Adults must live and function in an increasingly complex world; to do so requires a continual effort to find contexts that help to bring structure and order out of what William James described as a "buzzin', bloomin' confusion." The search for meaning is integral to all learning, especially for adults, who must be able to make sense out of the overload of information to which they are constantly exposed.

Since each person's experience is unique, learning that is experiential emphasizes individuality. Thus, traditional education is subject-centered, but nontraditional education is learner-centered and the effective teacher of adults is more concerned with assisting learners toward positive change than with advancing a particular discipline. Adult learners favor interdisciplinary or multidisciplinary approaches that help them overcome fragmentation by developing connections among phenomena.

The characteristics of experiential learning, as expressed in the writings of Carl Rogers, are:

There is a quality of personal involvement.
It is self-initiated.
It is pervasive.
It is evaluated by the learner.

Here the learner's role is so pivotal that Rogers goes so far as to state that we cannot teach other individuals directly, but can only facilitate their learning.

WHY ADULTS LEARN

The question of *how* adults learn is also linked to *why* they learn. In the previous chapter, we mentioned some of the benefits adults hope to gain from their studies, but adult motivation is too various to be contained in any list. Ask ten adult learners why they are studying and you may receive ten different reasons. An ambitious effort to classify and analyze adult learning motivation was begun by Cyril Houle in the 1950s at the University of Chicago.[4] He discovered three broad categories of learners that reveal a relationship between the how and why of adult learning:

1. Goal-oriented learner. This type is characterized by discontinuity. Learning takes place in response to a perceived need or interest. Individuals in this group apply themselves intensively as long as the need or interest is present; when they

have achieved a specific goal, they tend to discontinue their studies until another goal asserts itself.

2. Activity-oriented learner. Learning is fostered in a social context, through relationships with other learners. Learners in this group are enthusiastic participators.

3. Learning-oriented learner. Such a learner seeks knowledge for its own sake. As contrasted with the first group, this group tends to pursue learning in a steady flow. Learning-oriented learners are highly receptive to conceptual approaches.

In continuing Houle's research at the Ontario Institute for Studies in Education, Allen Tough found that adults tend to organize their learning around projects, for example, becoming a better parent or building a boat.[5] Here again, the adult learner demonstrates a need to apply what is learned and to seek meaning, purpose, and action in learning, as in Houle's first two categories. Says Patricia Cross in *Adults as Learners:* "Adult learners are frequently motivated by the pragmatic desire to use or apply the knowledge or skill. Most often, they hope to take action—do something, produce something, or decide something."[6]

THE LIFE CYCLE AND THE ADULT LEARNER

Our understanding of how and why adults learn has been profoundly influenced by recent research on the life cycle. The major credit for altering social attitudes toward adulthood in this century belongs to Charlotte Bühler, Erik Erikson (1963), and, more recently, Roger Gould (1978) and Lissy Jarvik. Spurred by the vastly increasing number of people now living into old age, their research has brought fresh perceptions to adult learning by demonstrating that growth and development take place on a continuum, that human life is cyclical, with regularities and transitions occurring throughout the life span.

A cyclical view of human development challenges the traditional emphasis on youth as the most favorable time for learning; instead, each stage of life is seen as having its own value and its own tasks to accomplish. As Alan Knox puts it, "A life-span view of development includes attention to openness, flexibility, creativity and choice at each stage of the adult life cycle."[7] Life stages or transitions serve as triggers for learning, helping individuals to work their way toward higher stages of development. This interactionist approach to adult development is seen in Erik Erikson's charting of eight successive life stages (Figure 2.1).

LIFE STAGES AND CAREER EDUCATION

The developmental perspective has also been finding its way into changing ideas about work and careers. Underlying these changes is the emerging concept of a shift from a linear to a cyclical life plan. In the linear plan, education is for the

FIGURE 2.1   The Interplay of Successive Life Stages

	1	2	3	4	5	6	7	8
H. Old age								Integrity vs. despair, disgust: *Wisdom*
G. Maturity							Generativity vs. self-absorption: *Care*	
F. Young adulthood						Intimacy vs. isolation: *Love*		
E. Adolescence					Identity vs. identity confusion: *Fidelity*			
D. School age				Industry vs. inferiority: *Competence*				
C. Play age			Initiative vs. guilt: *Purpose*					
B. Early childhood		Autonomy vs. shame, doubt: *Will*						
A. Infancy	Trust vs. mistrust: *Hope*							

Adapted from Erik Erikson, *Childhood and Society*, Norton, New York, 1963.

young, work for the middle-aged, and leisure for the elderly. The cyclical life plan redistributes education, work, and leisure over the life span.[8] Even within the linear plan, which is still in effect for most people, careers increasingly are being seen from a developmental view. Career educators adopting this view have discovered four basic patterns for men and for women (Table 2.1).[9] Continuous careers (the conventional and stable) are found mainly among the skilled, clerical, executive, and professional fields. The discontinuous (unstable, multiple-trial, and interrupted) are more common among men and women at the lower socioeconomic levels, in the unskilled, semi-skilled, and, to a lesser degree, clerical and sales.[10]

Career education and guidance generally have been based on the assumption that most people pursue continuous, either stable or conventional careers. Since there is mounting evidence that this is not true for most adults, teachers and counselors in career education can expect, in the years ahead, to be engaged in preparing students for discontinuity, for change both predictable and unpredictable.

ADULT INTELLIGENCE

In altering our view of adulthood, life-cycle theorists have also sharply revised earlier assumptions regarding the decline of intelligence and learning capacity in

TABLE 2.1.   Career Patterns[9]

Stage	Characteristics
	Male Career Patterns
Conventional	Some change, followed by stability
Stable	Entry into an occupation after finishing training and remaining in it
Unstable (serial)	Alternating periods of stability and change which may be long and infrequent
Multiple-trial	Frequent change and short periods in any one occupation
	Female Career Patterns
Conventional	Homemaking after a period of paid work
Stable	Homemaking instead of paid work or paid work in only one occupation
Interrupted	Paid work, then homemaking, and again paid work
Double-track	Simultaneous paid work and homemaking (becoming more common today)

adults. Educational psychologists make a distinction between "crystallized" and "fluid" intelligence in the maturing individual which is important for teachers and others working with adults.

Crystallized intelligence is related to experience; fluid intelligence is based on biological forces. Extensive testing shows a similarity between the "fluid" curve and the old cross-sectional one—peaking in the midtwenties and then declining. The "crystallized" curve shows no sign of declining; instead, it continues rising to the end of life. In experience-related education, at least, mature adults have a clear advantage over the young.

MEASURING ADULT INTELLIGENCE

At the present time, there is no reliable instrument or efficient procedure to measure adult intelligence. The most widely used test is the Wechsler Adult Intelligence Scale (WAIS), which was designed to provide a general assessment of ceiling performance by adults on tests of mental ability. Though these tests are regarded as helpful in providing a rough estimate of adult ability to perform verbal learning in educational settings, they are less useful in relating learning to social effectiveness, as, for example, in job performance or culinary accomplishment.

There is, in fact, growing skepticism, about the usefulness of intelligence tests as determinants of mental ability. Critics point out that the tests are culture-bound, reflecting the values of the tests' creators. Applied to adults, they bypass the rich inventory of knowledge and skills acquired through life experience. Commenting on what individuals know at fifty that they do not know at twenty, Adlai Stevenson said, "The knowledge acquired with age is not a knowledge of formulas or forms of words, but of people, places, actions—a knowledge gained by touch, sight, sound, victories, failures, sleeplessness, devotion, love—the human experience and emotions of this earth and of one's self and others.' (John MacLeish, *The Ulyssean Adult,* p. 126)

LEFT BRAIN, RIGHT BRAIN

In the light of recent research on the left and right brain hemispheres which locates analytical thinking in the left hemisphere and intuition and insight in the right, Stevenson's comments could be interpreted as favoring right-brain activity. Certainly, the emphasis in American education has been on the analytical, and most of the intelligence-measuring instruments have been designed to gauge left-brain activity, intuition and insight being far more difficult to measure. As Abraham Maslow and others have pointed out, this emphasis has excluded vast areas of knowledge and accomplishment that flow from "the human experience and emotions of this earth," particularly those associated with the training and experience of women.[11] In teaching adults, an important goal is the achievement of balance between the two kinds of mental activity. Carl Sagan says:

> The most significant creative activities of our or any other human culture—legal and ethical systems, art and music, science and technology—were made possible only through the collaborative work of the left and right cerebral hemispheres. . . . The creative act has major right-hemisphere components. But arguments on the validity of the result are largely left-hemisphere functions.[12]

ADULT LEARNING CAPABILITY

In the absence of precise measuring techniques, there exists today a store of information about adult learning capability, much of it emanating from experience and observation, that offers valuable cues to teachers and other practitioners working with adults. Some fundamental principles that can be extracted from this body of knowledge are as follows:

When they can control the pace of their learning, adults in their forties and fifties have about the same learning ability as they had in their twenties or thirties. There is some evidence of decline in learning ability from the sixties onward; however, this decline may be due to factors other than age, such as poor health or the emotional and financial problems connected with retirement or with the death of a spouse. Dr. Lissy Jarvik, a professor of psychiatry at UCLA who has been studying the matter for many years, found that, under reasonably normal conditions, there is no decline in ability even into the seventies and eighties,[13,14]

Learning ability is more consistently associated with social class and educational background than with age. The more education an individual has had, the more likely it is that he or she will be able to achieve a high standard of intellectual performance. The correlation between educational opportunities and income level shows up in the composition of the adult audience, which includes a disproportionate number of those in higher-than-average income brackets.

Learning in the middle and later years is closely related to adaptability. A decline in adaptability is fairly common to people in their midyears, who often find it difficult to make adjustments to new and unfamiliar situations.

In the broadest sense, the learning process takes the same course in all human beings regardless of age or cultural background. There are certain requisites for learning whether the student is a child in elementary school or a middle-aged adult taking courses in university extension. Of these, the most important are curiosity, motivation or the will to learn, and the drive to achieve. The individual who possesses none of these is unlikely to progress much beyond mechanical, rote learning, and the teacher who attempts to work with such students will find it a frustrating and unrewarding task.

Mental development also reveals basic similarities in both adults and children. It is not a steady accretion moving along a predictable upward slope, but a matter of leaps forward followed by periods of rest and consolidation. The leaps ahead seem to be stimulated by the development of certain capacities that have to ripen before others can begin to grow; these leaps appear to be related to environment rather than to age.

In what respects does age affect the individual's ability to learn? From a developmental perspective, physiological changes appear to be less influential than psychological needs and drives. Comparing adult and young students: The fourteen- to sixteen-year-old is preoccupied with peer group relations, school relationships, bodily concerns, the opposite sex. In the Eriksonian scheme, the interplay at this adolescent stage is between identity and identity confusion and the special task or goal is fidelity. The seventeen- to nineteen-year-old is concerned with school as a stepping-stone to a career, with friends, sex, plans for the future, independence, mobility, social issues. Nineteen to twenty-two is a time for leaving school, or continuing with graduate studies, starting a career, finding a mate. Industriousness vies with feelings of inferiority as the young man or woman strives toward competence.

During these years, the student is learning within prescribed limits, studying what is assigned, and, in the average institution, adjusting to rigid structures and patterns. Lacking experiential reference points, the student relies on the institution for guidance as he or she moves along in lockstep progression toward the goal of a degree or credential that is expected to bring material advancement. Learning is accomplished through testing, grading, competition; intelligence is equated with performance. There is little room left for what Thorstein Veblen called the "idle pursuit of curiosity" or for "intrinsic" learning, for which there are no external rewards.

The adult in the middle years is responding to a special set of needs and conflicts. The middle years are a time of responsibility, of caring for others—in many cases, both aging parents and children moving toward or already in the stage of young adulthood. In today's view of aging, these years are "the new middle age," spanning young adulthood and old age and offering a potential for productivity that was not available to most people in previous eras.[15] In normal psychological development, identity confusion has given way to a growing sense of self-awareness. Adults in midlife have amassed sufficient experience to draw upon for self-appraisal, which can help to steer them through the emotional disruptions and crises of this time.

Feelings of inferiority may persist, but they are likely to become more manageable. "It took me all this time," people in their forties and fifties often say, "to reach the point where I don't care what others think of me. I'm more concerned with what I think of myself."

Jung describes this feeling as the growth of "individuation," a developmental process through which the adult becomes authenticated, more intensely aware of his or her uniqueness. If this awareness is encouraged and channeled into productive pursuits, the individual can become a more autonomous, more active human being. It is not uncommon to see at this time a resurgence of spontaneity, of that free expression that is often present in the child and suppressed as social roles and approved modes of behavior are imposed by a succession of institutional pressures: family, church, school, workplace.

We should make a distinction at this point between adulthood and maturity. The dictionary definition of "maturity" is "full development," a condition that is not automatically guaranteed by the accumulation of birthdays. Psychological age need not correspond with chronological age. As Binet demonstrated when, at the turn of the century, he set out to measure the intelligence of children, a child may be eight years old chronologically and five or twelve years old psychologically. A man of thirty-five may have the ego-centered outlook of a five-year-old. A woman of forty-eight may have retained the identity confusions and insecurities of her teens. Since the primary task of the teacher is to assist the process of growth, it would obviously be a boon for teachers of adults to be able to detect immaturities in their students. Are there reliable criteria of maturity? In his classic work *The Mature Mind,* Harry Overstreet identified several characteristics of mature individuals:

> They are life-affirming, living as fully as their personal resources allow, continually strengthening their linkages with life.
>
> They are aware of their uniqueness and special aptitudes and are applying these individual powers constructively, in their personal, occupational, and community lives.
>
> They are open to the world about them and are constantly striving to learn and improve their competence; they are never satisfied that their present store of knowledge and skill is sufficient.
>
> Their power over their environment is matched by a growing awareness of what is involved in what they do, how their behavior affects others.
>
> They accept the fact that, although they are unique, they are also members of a family, community, nation, and beyond that, are part of the universal human experience.
>
> They accept responsibility for their own actions and do not rely on scapegoats, alibis, or coverups.[16]

These criteria describe an individual who is self-aware, self-directed, and actively engaged with his or her environment. Immaturity in adults frequently manifests itself as passivity. As a result of social conditioning, of the failure of their earlier education to encourage independent thinking, many adults act out their lives according to standards of behavior established for them by various "authorities." There are the "experts" who, through their specialized knowledge, become a kind of priesthood and whose decisions—legal, medical, technological —are accepted unquestioningly. There are the "therapies" that promise instant solutions to all human problems and guaranteed success in sexual, social, financial, and other activities. There are charts that determine behavior according to the position of the stars at the moment of birth. And there are those pervasive authorities who wear such labels as "common sense," "normalcy," "public opinion," "human nature," "bureaucratic efficiency," and "heredity."

Adults who are accustomed to accept unthinkingly the ideas and opinions of external authorities will expect the teacher to serve as a guru, providing them with prepackaged information or skills that will automatically meet their needs and solve their problems. The teacher who assumes this role with adult students will be shortchanging the teaching-learning process. In place of a mutually enriching, shared experience, in which there are gains on both sides, the relationship will be one in which the students will remain passive receivers while the teacher carries the entire burden of whatever learning takes place. Much of this learning, however, will have little value for today's adult learner. To be an effective teacher of adults requires an understanding of how adults learn, what their special learning problems are at different stages of their lives, and how to help them integrate living and learning.

CRITERIA FOR ADULT LEARNING

Adults respond positively to learning when:

the information has some personal meaning for them

they can relate what they are studying to their learning goals

they are active participants in the learning process

they are exploring new information and experience

the learning sessions are uninterrupted and extend over a substantial span of time: a two-hour seminar once a week is more beneficial than three weekly fifty-minute sessions

they can consolidate what they have learned before going on to new information or skills

they receive feedback during learning, thus avoiding the problem of unlearning: for this reason, the lecture-discussion that provides an opportunity to ask questions along the way is preferable to the lengthy lecture

they can learn in an unpressured, noncompetitive environment

REFERENCES

1. Malcolm Knowles, *The Adult Learner: A Neglected Species,* Gulf Publishing Co., Houston, 1973.
2. Quoted in Paolo Freire, *Education for a Critical Consciousness,* Seabury Press, New York, 1973, p. 36.
3. James W. Botkin, Mahdi Elmandjra, and Mircea Malitza, *No Limits to Learning,* Report to the Club of Rome, Pergamon Press, Elmsford, N.Y., 1979, p. 8.
4. Cyril Houle, *The Inquiring Mind,* University of Wisconsin Press, Madison, Wisc., 1961.
5. Knowles, op. cit.
6. K. Patricia Cross, *Adult Learners,* Jossey-Bass, San Francisco, 1981, p. 84.
7. Alan B. Knox, *Adult Development and Learning,* Jossey-Bass, San Francisco, 1981, p. 13.
8. Cross, op. cit.
9. Donald E. Super, *Career Education and the Meaning of Work,* U.S. Department of Health, Education, and Welfare, Washington, D.C., June 1976, pp. 26–27.
10. Super, op. cit.
11. Abraham H. Maslow, *Toward a Psychology of Being,* Van Nostrand, Princeton, 1968.
12. Carl Sagan, *The Dragons of Eden,* Random House, New York, 1977, p. 185.

13. Lissy F. Jarvik, Carl Eisdorfer and June Blum eds. *Intellectual Functioning in Adults: Psychological and Biological Influences,* Springer Publishing, New York, 1973.
14. Lissy F. Jarvik, ed. *Aging into the 21st Century: Middle Ages Today,* Gardner Press, New York, 1978.
15. Anne Simon, *The New Years: A New Age,* Alfred Knopf, New York, 1968.
16. Harry Overstreet, *The Mature Mind,* Norton, New York, 1949.

Chapter 3

SPECIAL LEARNING PROBLEMS OF ADULTS

We've observed that, in some respects, the experience of learning is similar for adults and children, but we've also seen that there are important differences between adults and children as learners. "Adults are not merely tall children," Jane Zahn notes. "They have different body characteristics, different learning histories, different reaction times, different attitudes, values, interests, motivations and personalities. Therefore, those who are trying to help adults learn must be aware of these differences and adjust teaching and the learning environment accordingly."[1]

Malcolm Knowles has suggested that, to emphasize the distinction between learning by adults and learning by children, in adult education the term "pedagogy" be discarded in favor of "andragogy." "Pedagogy," from the Greek, is made up of the stem *paid* for "child" and *agogus* for "teacher of," the literal translation being "teacher of children." "Andragogy," with its prefix from the stem *andr*, meaning "man," is offered as a more appropriate term for adult learning.*

The following table sets forth the differing assumptions upon which pedagogy and andragogy are based:

*Since "andr-" refers to man literally as "male", it would seem that "anthropagogy", the stem "anthr-" referring to "humankind" would be even more appropriate.

	PEDAGOGY	ANDRAGOGY
Self-concept	Dependence	Self-direction
Primary learning resources	Teacher's knowledge and authority	Learner's experience and motivation
Learning orientation	Subject -oriented	Problem-oriented

The implication to be drawn from this contrast is that the principal task of the teacher of adults is to help learners become self-directed. This is a challenging task since, as Knowles observes, "by and large, the adults we work with have not learned to be self-directing inquirers; they have been conditioned to be dependent on teachers to teach them. And so, they often experience a form of culture shock when first exposed to truly adult programs."[2]

THE FIVE PROBLEM AREAS

In addition to encountering culture shock, adults experience special learning problems in attempting to master new information or skills. These difficulties can generally be attributed to five factors: the conditions under which adults learn, psychological barriers to learning, memory difficulties, poor study habits, and lack of basic skills, particularly in mathematics and language.

Learning Conditions

As an increasing number of women enter the work force, and as the mandatory retirement age is extended, the proportion of adult learners who are working is expanding accordingly. College and university extension divisions have felt the effects of this development in the decline in enrollment in their daytime classes and the stepped-up interest in career education. For the teacher of adults, the fact that most of the people in your class have been working at jobs during the day has certain important implications for the teaching-learning transaction.

Heading the list is the fact that you are dealing with people who are not at the top of their energies. A typical student—let's say, a woman with two school-age children and a full-time job—is attending your class after a day that started early in the morning and probably included driving children to school, putting in eight hours on the job, stopping on the way home to shop for groceries, preparing dinner for the family, driving to class, and finding a parking spot. It takes a high level of commitment and motivation—which, fortunately most adults students have—to spend the evening studying after a busy, pressured, energy-consuming day.

The principal effects on learning of adult learning conditions are:

Short concentration span
Fatigue
Resistance to new information
Low level of initiative and participation

Instructional strategies are:

Avoid long lectures. Break up material into mini-lectures of ten to fifteen minutes
    duration.
Plan for lively, meaningful tasks and activities.
Provide for variety in methods and materials; for example, follow a verbal exercise
    with an audiovisual presentation or a role-playing activity.
Introduce new information by establishing connections with prior learning.
Allow at least one ten-minute break for each class hour.
Arrange for good lighting, acoustics, room temperature, and ventilation to minimize
    fatigue and strain.
Involve students in identifying objectives and procedures.

Counselors or teachers should discourage a prospective student from taking on
a course when considerable out-of-class work is required at a time when the
student's life is already overloaded with responsibilities and burdens. Adults who
attempt to take on more than they can handle may be setting up conditions in
which their efforts to progress toward their learning goals are frustrated. They
are better off postponing their study plans until a time when the load has been
lightened; they might be spared a failure that could act as a permanent brake on
their learning aspirations.

Psychological Barriers

Many adults, particularly those who have been out school for some time, suffer
from a lack of confidence in their ability to learn and perform well in the student
role. They worry about their ability to take notes, write papers, pass exams, and
keep up with others in the class. They are anxious about finding time to do
homework and carry out projects requiring time-consuming research. Their concerns may emanate from a shaky sense of self and a fear of being "shown up"
by the instructor or by better-prepared classmates.

Some of these anxieties have their origin in unhappy school experiences during
the growing-up years. "It took me a long time to make up my mind to become
a student again," confesses a woman enrolled in a management certificate program. "I had this teacher in high school whom I will never forget. For some
reason, I became a target for his hostility, and he never missed an opportunity

to belittle or disparage me. The experience was so painful, I decided not to go on to college and I really needed all my courage to enroll in this program."

Also fairly common among adult students are feelings of guilt, particularly when the time used for studying is taken away from other duties and responsibilities. Women are more likely to experience home-related guilt, the sense that they are spending time and money on themselves which, they may have been led to believe, properly belong to their family. Both men and women are vulnerable to the feeling that studying in maturity, particularly when it is purely for enjoyment, is a form of self-indulgence. This attitude, a vestige of that early period when adult education was considered a frivolous pursuit, has not yet entirely disappeared.

A third psychological barrier for mature people is the development of a "mind-set." Once this type of inflexibility takes hold, according to Simone de Beauvoir, people "are most reluctant to let it go. Even when they are faced with problems to which the mindset no longer has the least reference, they still cling to it."[3] A mindset makes it more difficult for adults to master a foreign language or deal with a new symbol system—molecular physics, for example. Once the mental barrier has been breached, with the help of a skillful teacher, the adult's self-confidence begins to build and the mindset gradually gives way to an exhilarating sense of accomplishment. Mature learners are continuously demonstrating their ability to master new and complex material. A celebrated instance is journalist I. F. Stone, who became a Greek scholar in his seventies.

The principal effects on learning of psychological barriers are:

Poor attendance: absences tend to coincide with dates of scheduled exams, delivery of term papers, or any form of presentation before class
Resistance to unfamiliar material
Nonparticipation as a form of self-protection
Tendency to keep instructor and classmates at a distance

Instructional strategies are:

As far as possible, remove doubt and uncertainty from the learning situation. Using a technique called "contracting," advise students of requirements and responsibilities at the first session. Credit students should be informed of any special requirements they will be expected to fulfill.
Always provide feedback on homework and exams, but do so privately through written comments. Criticism should be offered in a constructive and sympathetic manner.
Design examinations as part of the learning process, not merely to assign grades. Make sure the grading system is clearly understood and adhered to. Encourage self-testing and self-evaluation.
Promote interaction between yourself and students and among the students in as many ways as possible. Role-playing exercises and group projects are effective strategies for interactive learning.
Make abundant use of the three Rs: recognition, reinforcement, reward.

In the long run, psychological barriers are overcome through the learning experience itself. If you can encourage adult learners to continue their education, they will gradually shore up and strengthen their personal resources and progress toward their learning goals with greater self-assurance.

Memory Difficulties

The function of memory in learning is complex and controversial. How important is it to be able to retain large chunks of information? Does memory decline appreciably with age? Since the fear of memory loss is one of the most inhibiting factors for adult leaners, these are key questions for teachers of adults; however, the subject of memory in relation to maturity has become so overlaid with myth and misinformation that until now it was difficult to lay hold of any hard-and-fast answers. Thanks to the recent growing interest in aging, some useful data are beginning to emerge.

In analyzing how memory works, researchers find there are three phases:

1. Registration: the electrochemical process by which information is encoded in the brain
2. Retention: the persistence or decay or neural traces that are encoded through registration
3. Recall: the searching or retrieval process by which the individual recovers the information, which is what we refer to as "remembering"

With advancing age, there appears to be some loss of registration, a decline in the individual's ability to encode the information to which he or she is exposed. It is possible that this is due to the breakdown which occurs when visual information is converted into its auditory form for memory storage, an important point to keep in mind when using visual aids. It has been fairly well determined, for example, that visual materials are more effective when supported by commentary, readings, or both.

Interestingly, it is the retention rather than the registration phase that is most troublesome for adult learners, among whom a common complaint is, "No matter how hard I try to retain information, I can't seem to do it." The prevailing notion is that this type of memory loss is an inevitable accompaniment of aging. It is often regarded as a sign of senility. Some gerontologists, though, are far from convinced that this is the case. Dr. Lissy Jarvik, a Los Angeles psychiatrist who has been conducting research into the aging process for many years, suggests that memory problems in mature people may result from a combination of faulty learning and conformity to age stereotyping.

Both retention and recall show a remarkable improvement when the information is meaningful. Most of us know from our own experience that we have little trouble remembering what we want to and need to know. This does not mean, however, that we can absorb only that which is narrowly related to our immediate, day-by-day concerns. The creative teacher is able to expand the student's needs and interests so that an ancient Chinese poem or an expressionist painting can take on a directness and relevance for the individual which they did not have before.

The entire question of memory as a function of learning is being reassessed today in view of technological developments and evolving theories of learning. How important, to return to one of our earlier questions, is memorization when we have such technologies as computers and microfilm for the storage and retrieval of information? Doesn't the "knowledge explosion" that characterizes the world of today and surely the world of tomorrow call for the ability to retrieve and utilize information rather than to store it in the human mind?

Posing questions like these sets up a formidable challenge to methods and procedures that are among the sacred cows of American education. Memorizing has always been central to the "hole-in-the-head" theory of learning, which represents a view of education

as if it were some process by which an entrance is somehow forced into the brain and facts are poured or stamped in. The process is seen as a simple one. Organize your facts carefully; use repetition and other devices to make sure that they are properly injected into the mind. One concomitant of this notion is that the heads and minds of children are regarded as easier to penetrate, as less cluttered than those of adults.[4]

The hole-in-the-head approach can be observed in any number of classrooms throughout all levels of education. It presupposes a passive student–active teacher relationship and, especially in colleges and universities, favors the lecture method, through which students take in certain prescribed quantities of information in order to regurgitate much of this at exam time.

For teachers of adults, such methods as the hole-in-the-head, essentially exercises in memorizing, are not likely to produce the best results. Memory has its place in learning, regardless of the student's age, but it should be brought into balance with other elements in the learning process.

Principal effects on learning of memory difficulties are:

Errors of omission (forgetting) rather than commission (making mistakes)
Examination phobia
Inability to organize information

Instructional strategies are:

Pace each learning session to allow student to proceed at a rate that permits mastery
of the material.

In presenting new material, provide aids—charts, tables, associative concepts—to
help the student relate and organize the material for easier and more complete
recall.
Provide sufficient time and opportunity for practice.
Give short, frequent quizzes rather than one or two major examinations.
Wherever appropriate, place more emphasis on the skills of locating and utilizing
information than on mechanical memorization.

Poor Study Habits

Teachers of adults are frequently baffled by the student who starts out so promis-
ingly, exuding energy and enthusiasm, taking an active part in classwork—and
then suddenly seems to lose interest and either drops out of the class or performs
so poorly that the experience has clearly been of little value. There may be several
explanations for this pattern of behavior: personal or family problems; health
problems, particularly the onset of such age-related physiological conditions as
loss of vision or hearing; emotional disturbance; a threatening situation at work.
Adult life is constantly vulnerable to problems and pressures that, when they
become serious enough, can disrupt learning. More commonly, though, the expla-
nation can be found in the adult's difficulty in developing productive study habits.

Adults who have been away from the classroom for some time tend to panic
at the thought of studying and taking exams. They are not sure how to go about
taking notes, reading for comprehension, preparing for examinations, using such
resources as libraries and language labs. Many adults are not really clear about
what it means to study. They may not have developed good study habits in their
earlier student days, and now they find themselves handicapped and poorly
equipped to accomplish what they have set out to do.

Fortunately, there are a number of helpful books available which deal with the
techniques of studying (see Bibliography, p. 111). Also, the teacher should make
sure the students understand what studying is, a procedure an individual uses to
comprehend and master a given amount of material in such a way that he or she
develops greater competence with that material. Studying involves four stages:

1. Gathering information (through reading, listening, observing, etc.)
2. Organizing information (arranging and categorizing disparate pieces of informa-
    tion)
3. Summarizing information (reducing to essentials, forming concepts around these
    basic elements)
4. Storing the information in such a way that it can be drawn upon when it is needed
    in the future

The teacher should impress upon students that working hard and working well
are not necessarily one and the same. An often heard comment from students is,

"I don't understand it. I'm working so hard and I'm not doing well." Your students should realize right from the start that studying requires discipline and hard work. If they have the idea that it is all fun and games, they are in for a letdown that may frustrate their learning and your teaching efforts.

Principal effects on learning of poor study habits are:

Fragmentation; difficulty in making associations
Erratic, inconsistent performance in class and/or on examinations
Loss of interest; inattention
Frustration; discouragement.

Instructional strategies are:

Include in introductory session a discussion of the importance of study habits; list
   recommended readings on blackboard or add to course bibliography.
From time to time, remind students of need to practice good study habits, to establish
   a schedule with fixed periods for study, to arrange for suitable study space at home.
Be alert to symptoms (learning effects) of poor study habits and try to pinpoint
   causes. If symptoms persist, recommend counseling.

Basic Skills

Not surprisingly, adults who are new to the experience of studying are often weak in basic skills: reading, writing, and mathematics. Many adults do not realize that these skills are specialized for studying and that, like a set of mechanical tools, they grow rusty with disuse. You may find yourself working with adults who hold or have held responsible jobs, involving large amounts of reading and writing— memos, correspondence, reports, as well as budgetary tasks—yet whose reading, writing, and mathematical abilities are not adequate for effective performance as learners.

A fifty-five-year-old retired businessman, returning to college, was stunned when his first history research paper was returned to him with a grade of C and the teacher's comment, "poorly organized; indicates inadequate comprehension of assigned readings." The businessman had been a voracious reader all his life and prided himself on his ability to write clearly; but in fact, his reading had been mainly for relaxation and his writing had been confined to business memos and letters, a form of communication very different from a research paper.

Adults who have been away from a structured learning situation for any length of time often need a period of retooling. They need practice in note taking, speedreading, spelling, and vocabulary building and, where relevant to their studies, in mathematics. They should realize that being a successful student, like playing a good game of tennis, requires constant practice, that their need to upgrade their verbal and numerical skills is no reflection on their intelligence or capability.

Principal effects on learning of inadequate skills are:

Difficulty with comprehension
Inability to keep up with reading assignments
Inadequate performance in writing assignments
Inability to handle math problems at even a simple level
Reluctance to participate in classwork for fear of revealing inadequacy

Instructional strategies are:

Lean heavily on repetition and review.
Assign exercises that require practice in use of skills.
Design quizzes and exams that require writing essays rather than answering true/-false or multiple-choice questions
Provide supports for students' self-esteem by noting and encouraging signs of progress.
Where progress is not forthcoming or is too slow, suggest that student enroll in one of the many study skills programs available at community colleges, extension divisions of four-year colleges and universities, and other adult education centers.

Remember that what most adults need, above all else, is to learn how to learn. Anything you can do to help them become more competent learners will enrich your teaching as well as their learning experience.

REFERENCES

1. Jane C. Zahn, "Differences Between Adults and Youth Affecting Learning," *Adult Education,* Winter 1967 Vol. XVIII no. 2, p. 67.
2. Malcolm Knowles, *The Adult Learner: A Neglected Species,* Gulf Publishing Co., Houston, 1973.
3. Simone de Beauvoir, *The Coming of Age,* Warner Books, New York, 1975, p. 34.
4. J. R. Kidd, *How Adults Learn,* Association Press, New York, 1973.

Chapter 4

CREATING A LEARNING ENVIRONMENT

Certain readily identifiable factors contribute to the environment in which the teaching-learning transaction takes place: the size of the class; the range of background and experience among the learners; the seating arrangement; the temperature and ventilation of the room; the availability of such requisite equipment as TV monitors, flip charts, and slide or film projectors in good working order. Above and beyond these logistic factors is the relationship between teacher and learner. The manner in which this relationship is established can make the critical difference between a good, bad, or indifferent teaching-learning experience. Much depends on the initial encounter between teacher and learners, at which each takes the measure of the other and impressions are formed that are often difficult to erase or modify later on.

THE FIRST ENCOUNTER

For the adult learner, the first session of a course, particularly of a noncredit course, is a shopping expedition. Even after poring over the attractively written copy in the catalog and seeking out information about the course and the instructor, adults are still likely to have questions about whether 'this is right for me" until that all-important first session. Unlike younger students in traditional learning situations, in which much of the curriculum is structured, adults are accustomed to having a wide range of choices, to weighing the pros and cons before making a decision, whether it is buying a car or planning a vacation trip or, as in this instance, choosing a course of study. Adult education, for the most part, offers the opportunity to pick and choose. In noncredit and in some areas of credit study, prospective students are self-selective, choosing this or that course, lecture series, or study tour in accordance with their tastes, needs, interests, limitations of time, and income.

In this sense, adult education is subject to market forces. Therein lies its challenge and frustration for the teacher. The fact that most of the students are there of their own free will puts teachers of adults on their mettle and is one of the principal reasons for the disorientation experienced by some academic faculty from traditional institutions, who are accustomed to students as a captive audience. Here, instead, the teacher confronts a group of people who can come and go pretty much as they please and who, even when they are seeking degrees, are looking for more than a piece of paper or parchment certifying completion of a course of study.

As self-selectors, what students will be looking for in the first session is a sign or clue that will either affirm or negate their choice, so that one of the first things you need to know is why they have chosen this class. There are several ways you can go about this, depending mainly upon the size of the class. If the class is small, no more than thirty students, the procedure can be quite informal. The sequence might go like this:

Step One: Introduce yourself. Add any personal statements that are relevant to the substance of the class. Suppose you are teaching a class in creative writing. In your introduction, you might share with the class a few autobiographical details:

"I have been a freelance writer for ten years—and the first few years, I collected enough rejection slips to paper a wall in my house. I learned the hard way what it takes to be a professional writer. Now that I'm being published more or less regularly, I want to share my experience with you in the hope of providing you with some practical help on the way to becoming a published writer."

In this way, you have briefly and effectively established your credentials in regard to the substance of the course and developed a link between your background and the learners' requirements. There is no need to go further at this time. Some teachers, particularly those with limited experience, feel that by becoming chatty and personal they are putting the students at their ease, "making them feel at home." Doing this tends to trivialize the teacher-learner relationship and fosters in the students the suspicion that their time is being wasted.

Step Two: Have the students introduce themselves and state their reason or reasons for enrolling in the class. (See "Needs Assessment" in Chapter 6.)

Step Three: Hand out your syllabus and bibliography and give the class a few minutes to look over these materials. Until they know what your plans are, they cannot be sure that the class will give them what they want.

Step Four: Make any explanatory comments about the syllabus and bibliography that may be necessary and add other pertinent information regarding breaks, class exercises, exams, special projects, field trips, guest speakers. Do not, however, overwhelm the class with plans and projects at this first encounter. Let them know that you are aware of their time pressures and that the design of the class will be a shared process. You are saying, in effect, that you have a plan for the class, but that it is not cast in concrete. You accept it as your responsibility to be prepared with a structure, but a flexible structure, and it is their responsibility to suggest any adaptations or revisions in the design that will increase its usefulness for them and bring it closer to their expectations.

Step Five: Invite comments on the plan that you have presented. Since students tend to be shy about expressing themselves at this first encounter, you should be prepared to offer some possible adaptations of your own in order to launch the discussion. Write all comments and suggestions offered by the class on the blackboard or flip chart. See that each one receives fair consideration. Evaluate with the class the suggestions offered, eliminating those that are impractical or too far from the purpose or goals of the course. In the creative writing class mentioned earlier, for example, the suggestion that "new journalism" be included might not be considered viable since this is a highly specialized area; however, the inclusion of a session or two on writing for children, if there is sufficient interest among members of the class, might be a logical and worthwhile expansion of the original course plan.

It should be recognized that the above procedure is not one that can be applied across the board. In certain courses and programs—in continuing education for the professions and other career and credit areas—the content and methodology are strictly mandated and there is little room for adaptation through the group process. In noncredit learning and other learning situations that allow for flexibility, though, the merging of learner interests and resources with the teacher's objectives can sharpen an instructional plan so that it works better for both teacher and learners.

In this first encounter, your object in making the class aware of learning as a shared process is to emphasize that there are certain responsibilities on both sides. You are responsible for organizing the information and materials of the course to correspond as closely as possible with the learners' needs and goals. They are responsible for making whatever modifications are necessary and practical in order to apply the content to their individual plans and purposes.

THE PERSONAL INTERACTION

In this first encounter, the students will be taking their measure of you as a teacher, looking for clues that will answer questions in their minds: Have you prepared for the class, or are you intending to "wing it?" Are you patient? Compassionate? Do you have a sense of humor? Are you fair? Do you have any strong biases or prejudices? Perhaps most important: Do you really enjoy teaching?

You, in turn, will have your antennae out, picking up signals from the class, making mental notes for future reference. Even in this initial meeting, it is possible to make some educated guesses about the people in your class. Over there is one who is likely to be troublesome: already, twenty minutes into the class, she has complained about the location of the classroom, the temperature, and the parking situation. You may find yourself singling out the class wise guy, the amateur psychologist, the cynic, the scoffer. Since people become individuated in maturity, almost any adult class is likely to represent a microcosm of the human species with all its foibles, flaws, and diversity. The tendency to label or classify— "cynic," "wise guy," etc.—should be firmly resisted, however, since it can desensitize you to the range of possibilities these adult students may possess behind what is often a protective facade and that you, the teacher, have the power to draw out.

The size of the class will, of course, have a direct relationship to the interaction between you and the students from the first session onward. As class size grows, it becomes more difficult to establish a warm, personal learning environment, but even in large-size classes, the teacher who is open and enthusiastic, knows and cares about the subject of the course, has the "human touch," and regards each member of the class as an interesting and important individual, can create an atmosphere in which the students feel comfortable and confident and are prepared to fulfill their responsibilities as learners.

DEVELOPING AN EGALITARIAN ATMOSPHERE

Since teachers of adults are human, it is to be expected that you will respond more positively to some people in your class than to others. You may even find yourself actively disliking a few—and there is every chance, as these things go, that the feeling will be mutual. Suppressing your feelings may be difficult, but it might be a good idea for you to analyze them and attempt to discover the cause. One instructor found that her hostility to a certain student could be traced to the fact that the student reminded her of her ex-husband; this insight helped her to overcome her negative feelings and deal with the student in a cordial manner.

Even if you are unable to conquer your dislike for one or more members of your class, it need not constitute a problem. Your manner should be friendly but impersonal, in line with the teacher-student relationships suggested in Chapter 1. A good host or hostess treats all guests courteously, even if there are some he or she prefers to others. Consultants try to do the best-possible job for their clients regardless of their personal feelings toward them. Partners, whether they like each other or not, know they must be mutually supportive if their enterprise is to succeed. The teacher's personal feelings toward students are simply irrelevant and have no more place in the teaching-learning transaction than the feelings of doctors toward their patients during the course of diagnosis and treatment. Playing favorites is almost invariably harmful to the sense of good fellowship in a class and marks you as lacking in objectivity and fairness.

Adult learners—particularly in today's social climate—are keenly sensitive to any hint of racial or sexist bias in an instructor. The instructor may be—often is—entirely unaware of such biases, but the class will pick up on them very quickly. Some "don'ts" to keep in mind:

Males
Don't address or refer to the women in your class as "ladies" or "girls" or comment
    on their personal appearance or mode of dress.
Don't tell jokes or anecdotes that stereotype women.
Don't use one tone of voice (businesslike, straight from the shoulder) for the men in
    your class and another (ingratiating, patronizing) for the women.

Both Sexes
Don't set lower standards for members of minority groups than for other students.
Don't forget that people from diverse cultural backgrounds have their own value
    systems which enter into their performance as learners.
Don't tell ethnic jokes.
Don't mispronounce students' names. If you have difficulty with a foreign spelling,
    ask the student for the correct pronunciation. (See Chapter 8, "Teaching Special
    Groups.")

These few simple principles can help to establish an egalitarian atmosphere in which all the individuals in the class feel comfortable with each other and with the teacher and are thus encouraged to learn to the limits of their potential. Does this mean that every learner must be dealt with exactly as every other learner? Not at all. The Orwellian statement that "some people are more equal than others" could have been inspired by a class of adult learners. The average adult class represents, as we have noted, a broad range of backgrounds, experiences, and capabilities. Teachers who are new to adult education often cite this diversity as their most difficult problem. How, they wonder, does one go about teaching a class in public relations, to take one example, when it includes people who are not quite sure what public relations is all about along with those who have had several years of experience in the field?

The most effective approach to this problem is to divide the class into groups according to level of background and experience and assign exercises and projects accordingly. Plan to intersperse group work with instructional modes appropriate for the class as a whole: simulation gaming, for example, or audiovisual presentations. Give as much individual attention as time and the class size permit to those students who have the most catching up to do. The point is not to try to equalize your students—this is neither possible nor desirable—but to create an ambience in which all have an equal chance to maximize their individual learning resources.

SEATING ARRANGEMENTS

The immovable seats, row upon row, that many of us remember from our school-days may well be the most disadvantageous arrangement ever devised for learning in a group. If this is the arrangement you must teach with, there is obviously nothing to do but make the best of it. Whenever possible, try to obtain a room with movable chairs, preferably those with armrests or other writing surfaces. There are any number of seating plans that can be used to encourage student participation and, in general, improve the flow of communication in the class. The following basic arrangements are suitable for most teaching situations and lend themselves to variations as required:

Seminar. Chairs are arranged in a circle around a table. Instructor's location is determined by the proximity of blackboard, flip chart, or audiovisual equipment. Usually not practical for more than twenty to twenty-five people.

Horseshoe. An oval arrangement with one side left open for instructor, guest speakers, or student presenters.

Rectangle. A variation on the seminar. May be used without tables if chairs have armrests or students have clipboards to write on. One side may be left open, as in the horseshoe format.

Small Groups. Chairs are arranged in several small circles or semicircles. Particularly useful for autonomous discussion groups.

With the help of a student or two, these seating plans should take no more than a few minutes to arrange at the start of a class. Seasoned instructors testify that it pays to devote some time and thought to the seating plan, since the physical arrangements of the room can have a significant influence on the learning environment.

THE SOCIAL FACTOR

There is an important dimension in adult education that has nothing to do with libraries or laboratories or the acquisition of information or skills. In our highly urbanized society, and with the breakdown of such institutions as the church and the extended family which provided opportunities for social contacts, some adults attend classes in continuing education primarily as a means of meeting people and alleviating loneliness. Educational purists tend to frown upon the mixing of socializing with studying. Considering the struggle adult education has had to achieve some measure of respectability in the educational establishment, one can understand the reluctance of practitioners to admit that adults may be impelled to become students for reasons other than intellectual curiosity or the desire to improve their financial condition. (It may be one of the vestiges of our Puritan ethic that makes cognitive and career development acceptable as educational motivations while downgrading the interpersonal aspects).

Nevertheless, the social dimension in adult education cannot be ignored and should be seen for what it is—a credit rather than a debit to the field. That there are people who come to your class mainly to meet other people should not have any effect upon the content or methodology of the course. It happens quite often, in fact, that adults who enroll in classes because, as one recently divorced man said, "it beats spending the evening watching TV," become dedicated learners. A woman who enrolled in a sociology class soon after being widowed reports that "I didn't even know what sociology was but I simply had to get out and mingle with people. Now I'm hooked on the subject and I'm back in college studying for my B.A. I hope to go on to graduate school and maybe a career in family counseling."

There are ways in which the social factor can be integrated into the learning process. One instructor who teaches the history of the American West in the extension division of a western university includes a picnic lunch at a historic site. She combines the lunch with a regular session of her class. An art teacher who is part owner of a local gallery makes it a point to invite his students to openings, at which there are refreshments and a partylike atmosphere. A teacher of interior design regularly schedules a house tour that culminates in a buffet dinner at his own home at which the class discusses the decor of the houses they visited. Imaginative flourishes such as these can be helpful in developing a congenial atmosphere and increasing the students' enjoyment of the class.

THE "HAPPINESS QUOTIENT"

Recognizing and capitalizing on the social dimension does not, however, require the teacher to provide "entertainment" for the students. Sometimes, in an effort to avoid boring the students, an instructor goes to the other extreme and attempts to raise the "happiness quotient" of the class through various diversions: amusing films that have no direct relevance to the course, guest speakers with a lively wit but little to say that enhances the course content, roleplaying or other exercises that do no not advance the goals of the course but are 'fun" for the students.

There are, of course, aspects of learning that cannot be made pleasurable—language drills, for example. If you have established a pleasant and productive learning environment, your class will find their entertainment in the learning itself: in the mastery of a foreign language, the discovery of a new idea, the development of new skills and competencies.

Chapter 5

TEACHING ROLES, STYLES, AND TECHNIQUES

A recent report on urban education programs revealed that the reason most teachers select a particular instructional approach is their familiarity with it.[1] In traditional education, a preference for the familiar has bred adherence to a fairly limited range of teaching methods, the one most commonly used being the lecture or lecture-discussion technique. Adult education, however, with its greater flexibility and diversity, has spawned a variety of instructional approaches that can provide a more versatile, more creative teaching-learning experience. In the course of this development, the range of roles available to the teacher has been greatly expanded.

We can identify two broad styles of instruction—proactive and reactive—that stem from two very different psychological bases. The proactive style is learner-centered and views learning as an individualized process of discovery and growth. In this mode, the learner takes the initiative and assumes primary responsibility for his/her education; the teacher acts as a facilitator or catalyst, taking cues from the learner's interests and objectives. Planning is an activity based on mutuality, on agreement between teacher and learner, and is essentially fluid and open-ended.

Reactive instruction places the learner in the position of responder. The teacher is the initiator and carries the major responsibility for whatever learning takes place. The assumption is that learners must, to some extent, be force fed (the hole in the head method). The teacher is planner, decision maker, final court of appeal. The learner reacts to the teacher's initiatives, plans, and decisions and relies on the teacher's assessment of his/her progress rather than on self-assessment.

THE PROACTIVE MODE

Many adults are the products of an educational system that has not encouraged a high degree of participation on the part of students. Consequently, the teacher of adults often finds that many in the class are not accustomed to taking an active part in the learning process. Shyness, the lack of self-confidence that is often characteristic of adult students, even fatigue can act as inhibitors.

How do you get through to those in the class who never ask a question, never make a comment, never volunteer or show any sign of initiative? The way you don't go about it is to single out these nonparticipators and make them the focus of attention as you try to draw them out. This method is virtually guaranteed to make them retreat even further into the background.

Encouraging Participation Through Group Discussion

Of the three principal proactive methods—group discussion, role playing, and independent study—the simplest and most effective as a means of encouraging participation is group discussion. There is something infectious about a lively discussion centering on a topic of common interest which acts as a magnet, attracting even the most withdrawn members of the class. As the discussion leader, your style and personality will have an influence on the structure and flow of the discussion, as will the relationships among members of the class. The leader must also be flexible, ready to adapt to varying situations. Though there are no surefire formulas, some general principles can guide you toward good class discussions and effective leadership.

To begin with, there must be something to discuss, and obvious though this factor may seem it is occasionally overlooked. Not all topics are discussable; a good discussion topic usually involves a variety of viewpoints. At times a discussion may develop spontaneously and move along on its own momentum, but what follows may be random talk, or what is known as a "pooling of ignorance." The definition of "discussion" is "to find out by examination"; in other words, discussion as distinguished from casual conversation is a *purposeful* activity. Therefore, the group should be given adequate preparation through a lecture, a film, or assigned readings so that each member is able to make an informed contribution to the argument or theme of the discussion.

On the other hand, this is not a decision-making process. It is a process of examination, an exploratory, open-ended procedure. A discussion may or may not precede the making of a decision, but in itself, it takes place without voting, consensus, or parliamentary rules.

Remember that a class or group is made up of individuals. Social psychologists may analyze "group behavior" and establish certain patterns of relationships that seem to characterize people in groups, but there is no evidence that a group is greater than or different from the sum of its parts. The group remains—or should remain—a loose collection of individuals. The discussion leader should avoid asking, "What does the group think?" Groups do not think unless they are manipulated. The question should be posed as "What do *you* think?"

As the discussion develops, the teacher (or group discussion leader, if someone other than the teacher is assigned to this role) should see to it that the purpose of the activity is not lost sight of or the class derailed by irrelevant information or personally directed remarks. An effort should be made to bring out as many different points of view as possible. If only one point of view is being expressed, ask the class to think of arguments that might be made for the other side. If other views are brought out in the assigned readings, use short excerpts for this purpose. Remember that there is no attempt to produce a single group answer to the issues being considered; the leader should never ask, "Don't you agree . . .?" but should continue to elicit individual views and reactions.

A good discussion will also be guided by sound reasoning, which includes four basic elements: *logic,* since no useful analysis can be built on fallacies; *semantics,* since the choice of words is essential for clarity and comprehension; *relevance,* or the weeding out of extraneous material; and *sequence,* the orderly and systematic development of an argument or idea.

The discussion leader should be careful not to provide answers or personal opinions. It may be difficult to remain impartial but there are good reasons for doing so:

> The prestige of your position as group leader may give your views more weight than anyone else's, and you will be using your position unfairly if you express your ideas.
> Once you become involved as a protagonist, expressing and defending your own views, you will not have time to perform the real functions of discussion leadership.

The discussion leader's tasks include:

1. Preparing for the meeting by mastering the basic material and as much additional material as possible.
2. Analyzing the material carefully and setting out the boundaries of the subject.
3. Defining the issues, with emphasis on those points on which there are likely to be divergent opinions.
4. Preparing questions. The question is the discussion leader's basic tool, and he or she should have several questions in mind at the start of the discussion. Questions should relate directly to the issues and should be brief and straightforward.
5. Opening the meeting. The leader's introduction should be brief and should set the stage for the discussion. This introduction may be followed by an opening question phrased to act as a trigger for the discussion. Additional questions may

be used to keep the discussion moving. Often the best questions arise from the discussion itself.

6. Encouraging participation. The leader should see to it that the more articulate members of the group do not monopolize the discussion. Those who are less verbal should be given every opportunity to get into the conversation, but this must be done tactfully and never by calling on them by name.

7. Bringing out all sides of the question. If only one point of view is being expressed, encourage participants to think of arguments on the other side even if they do not agree with them. The leader should be prepared to act as devil's advocate if necessary.[2]

With adequate information, a sense of purpose, and skilled leadership, a good discussion can motivate your students to become actively involved in the goals and activities of the class and in this way can help create an enjoyable and productive learning environment.

Role Playing

This technique has been in existence for many years. Conducting moot courts is a familiar feature of the law student's training, and mock political conventions and elections are long-established teaching devices in the social sciences. It is only in recent years, however, with the increasing emphasis on student participation, that role playing has developed as a method that can be used to achieve a variety of educational purposes. Educators recommend it as a means of helping adults to develop skills and behaviors for dealing with real-life situations.

Role playing can take various forms, from a simple improvisation to a complex simulation game or highly developed sociodrama. As an improvisation, it is most useful when it is important to the learning objectives of the learners to identify with a specific character, particularly one outside the range of their everyday experience. Suppose you are teaching a class in American history and you are in the Civil War period. What better way is there to have your students "get into the skin" of a Southern planter, a slave, a Union soldier, an abolitionist, the wife of a Confederate officer, and the like? The characters can be developed by teacher and students, working from assigned readings and class discussion. Each character should be clearly sketched in terms of personality, family background, and social setting.

Or let's say you are teaching a class in Assertive Communication for Women. The women in your class are aspirants for managerial jobs in large corporations. You consider it essential for them to understand and even empathize with the values and attitudes of the male executives who will be working with them. You realize, however, that it will be difficult to accomplish this goal by lecturing on the subject or even by attempting to generate a discussion; it would, after all, be unrealistic to expect the class in this case to be objective. You solve the problem by setting up a role-playing exercise in which the women in the class assume the role of the male personnel director. This exercise provides the basis for an analysis of the director's behavior and of the strategies available for dealing with it.

Role playing can take place with a group of any size, and the time required is anything from a few minutes to an entire class session. The class can be divided into "actors" and "audience," with the audience offering critiques of the role play. Time permitting, actors and audience should have an opportunity to change places in the course of the session.

As the facilitator, your responsibilities are:

1. To assist with structuring the role play and to be sure that the problem is clearly set out and placed in the appropriate context
2. To "stage-manage" the role play by outlining the scene, helping to arrange the physical setting, and responding to questions about the situation and characters
3. To probe the actors in regard to their thoughts and feelings during the course of the role play
4. To encourage the audience to comment and to promote discussion among actors and audience
5. To relate the role play to real-life experience
6. To bring the role play to an end if it appears to be generating tensions or getting off the track

Preparation

Although role playing is by its nature a spontaneous activity, it works best as a learning device when it is given a certain amount of structure. This can be very loose, but without some preplanning on the part of the teacher, the exercise may become so formless that its educational value is dissipated. In preparing for a role-playing exercise, the teacher should determine its goal and arrange for whatever charts or other supporting materials might be needed to facilitate the activity. It is often helpful to develop beforehand an opening question or challenge or a set of circumstances to set the role play in motion. You might launch the Civil War improvisation as follows: You are a plantation owner, deeply in love with your land, a compassionate human being who has always regarded your slaves as members of your family; one day, a runaway slave who has always been your favorite is caught and brought before you. How would you handle this situation?

Or in the class on Assertive Communication for Women, the opening question might be, How would you feel if, as a man who had achieved a middle-management position after twenty years of service to the company, a woman with less experience was brought in from outside and placed in a position as your supervisor? Allow some time for discussion of the characters, the setting, the emotions that are released by the situation. Be sure to allow sufficient time for the discussion following the role play, since this is the crucial part of the activity; it gives students an opportunity to analyze the feelings and attitudes brought out by the exercise and provides you with valuable feedback.

Simulation Gaming

This is an expansion of the role-playing technique which replicates a real-life system rather than an interpersonal encounter. Participants in the game assume the roles of decision makers and behave as they would in the real-life situation that is being simulated. As in any game, there are conventions that govern the activity. Ronald Hyman suggests these six:

1. Roles: The game assigns roles to the participants.
2. Rules: The rules hold only during the game sequence.
3. Goals: The goals of simulation games used in education are more complex and less explicit that those of such games as baseball or chess.
4. Rituals: There are certain behavior patterns which may not be related to the goals or rules but are necessary for the continuance of the game.
5. Language: Games have their own jargon, unrelated to the rules but important to the game.
6. Values: Each game has its own standards or criteria that are, of necessity, controlling.[3]

An example of a simulation game that has been used effectively in a program dealing with the judicial system is *You Are the Jury.* For this exercise, the teacher prepares a hypothetical case; members of the class assume roles as judge, defendant, prosecuting attorney, and defense attorney. (The instructor may take the role of the judge.) The rest of the class is divided into juries. A single jury may consist of as few as three or four members or as many as the class size permits. This exercise works best with several juries, but it can be conducted effectively with two or three.

The "case" is argued by the prosecutor and defense attorney, who have had an opportunity to prepare their arguments in advance. The judge explicates the legal issues, and the juries are then given a stipulated amount of time to deliberate and arrive at their decisions. A reporter from each jury now states the decisions arrived at and the reasoning that led to the ruling. A general discussion ensues as members of the different juries compare their decisions and reasoning. The instructor helps to keep the discussion moving and sees to it that the fundamental principles underlying the juries' decisions are clearly understood. A similar format was used in a conference on environmental education in which the planet Earth was cast in the role of plaintiff; prosecuting and defense attorneys presented arguments on both sides, and the audience as "juries" gave their verdicts after consideration of the arguments.

Sociodrama

A more elaborate version of the simulation game, sociodrama has been defined as a "re-creation of a dilemma in human relations through spontaneous and faithful enactment of the roles with accompanying feelings involved in the situation."[4] The class might act out the roles of senators arguing the pros and cons of a treaty banning nuclear weapons. Or they might simulate a group of futurists comparing and debating their projections for the years ahead. As compared with simulation gaming, sociodrama is less rule-bound and there are no specific goals aside from solving the problem.*

A few caveats about role playing in continuing education:

> As with any other teaching method, role playing should not be used indiscriminately. It works best in the social sciences and liberal arts, in which values play an important part, but it has only limited usefulness in teaching technical subjects.
> Some people in the class may be uncomfortable with role playing; they should not be forced to participate.
> Adults whose learning experience has been mainly in the reactive mode do not always take readily to role playing. Unfamiliarity has the same effect upon learners as upon teachers: they tend to doubt the seriousness of game playing and therefore tend to distrust it as a learning method. To overcome this negative bias the teacher may have to do a selling job, that is, spell out clearly the connection between the role play and the goals of the course. Also, throughout the exercise the teacher should be diligent in helping participants to maintain the focus of the simulation.

Advantages of Role Playing

When used appropriately, role playing has several advantages. It gives students an opportunity for interaction with each other. It provides a means for linking the topic that is being studied to the world beyond the classroom. Role playing is particularly useful as a device for investing abstract subject matter with the reality of day-to-day life, thus satisfying the student's need, especially strong among adults, for applied knowledge. In the simulation-game format, the analysis of possible moves and the possible consequences of those moves encourages critical thinking. Simulation games make it possible for the teaching-learning experience to take place on three levels at once. While participating, the student is (1) learning facts expressed in the context and dynamics of the game, (2)

---

*A useful reference is the *Handbook of Simulation Gaming in Social Education, Part 2: Directory,* published by the Institute of Higher Education Research, The University of Alabama.

learning the processes that are simulated in the game, (3) learning alternative strategies for decision making and problem solving.

INDEPENDENT STUDY

This method, by which the teacher works with the student on a one-to-one basis, has in the past played a marginal role in adult education, mainly in the form of correspondence study. With the recent development of open learning, generally known as the "university without walls," independent study is shedding its somewhat dowdy image and emerging in such attractive new guises as "contract learning" and "programmed instruction."

Contract Learning

The two major experiments with contract learning, both established with Ford Foundation funding, are The University Without Walls, a nationwide network of programs at twenty-nine colleges and universities, and Empire State College, a unit of the State University of New York. The basic feature of this mode of learning is the learning contract, which consists of a statement of long- and short-range goals, the topics of study, the resources to be used, the duration of study, and the means of evaluating the end product. The student's program is then structured as a series of contracts: written agreements as to what learning he or she will accomplish over the given period of time, specifying readings, research, writing, and any other work that will be performed in order to achieve the stated goals. Tests, grades, and credentials are not appropriate for contract learning. Instead, criteria for graduation are derived from the student's objectives.[5]

The function of the teacher in contract learning is to assist students in the design and evaluation of their projects. This is, obviously, very different from the traditional teaching style, and in recognition of this distinction, Empire State College coined a new term, "mentor," to describe a member of its faculty.

The mentor serves as the student's link with the college, helping the student deal with the complex tasks of assessment. Mentors routinely make a concerted effort to learn about each student's educational needs and background, an analysis that goes much further than the customary faculty advising function in many campus situations.

Comparing mentoring with traditional teaching, Sig Synnestvedt, dean of Empire State's Buffalo Learning Center, says "it's one thing to teach a class of thirty, but mentoring thirty students under this system requires the faculty member to sit eyeball to eyeball with a serious adult learner. There's no faking it or doing potted lectures. Some faculty members may experience real stress, and a few have scurried back to traditional teaching. Yet the rewards along this path are stunning. To see another human being not just learn your subject but develop into a fuller, better person under your stimulation and guidance happens only occasionally in the conventional course, but it occurs routinely around here."

The average age of the contract-learning student is thirty-five. Forty percent come from minority groups, and about 50 percent are women. Most hold full-time jobs. Nearly half are close to or below the poverty line. One of these students, a thirty-eight-year-old mother of four, describes her experience this way: "The first thing I learned about this program is that it started with me—not with some curriculum I had to fit into. Practically everything I've done in working towards the degree has been something I've wanted or needed to do, either for my personal or professional development."[6]

Programmed Instruction

The development of this form of individualized learning is credited to B. F. Skinner, who in 1954 recommended the use of "teaching machines" that, he said, "can bring one programmer into contact with an indefinite number of students. This may sound like mass production, but the effect upon each student is surprisingly like that of a private tutor."[7]

Programmed instruction is an individualized method: the student works individually with electronic, mechanical, printed, or multimedia materials that have been specifically prepared to provide instruction. The materials help students to pace their learning according to their individual capabilities.

The major advantage of programmed instruction in the teaching of adults is that, with the diversity of background and experience among adult students, each student can start at that point in the course of study where he or she is ready to proceed. The students can perform as individuals rather than as a group, and are therefore able to move along at their own pace. This same general approach also characterizes computer-assisted instruction, autotutorials, and courses by radio and television.

THE REACTIVE MODE

The lecture, which is the principal reactive technique, has a place in the education of adults principally as a conveyor of factual information. It is particularly appropriate for large-size groups and is therefore the mainstay of college and university continuing education divisions that serve major metropolitan areas.

As a learning vehicle, the lecture, like the little girl in the children's rhyme, tends to be either very, very good or else it is "horrid." There are brilliant lecturers who are able to inspire their students so that what would ordinarily be an exercise in passivity becomes a valuable learning experience. Such lecturers are few and far between; for the most part, long, uninterrupted lecturing is not a productive method for adult learning.

It has been estimated that the attention span of a typical adult learner attending a class at the end of a working day is anywhere from thirteen to fifteen minutes. After this span of time, the lecturer's voice registers as a steady drone that tends to have soporific effects.

The lecture, however, can be presented in a style that captures and holds the attention of the audience and promotes interaction. Variations and modifications that enrich and enliven the lecture include:

Breaking the lecture into minilectures running ten to fifteen minutes, with intervals
  for questions and discussion
Setting up a reaction panel to put questions to the speaker at scheduled intervals
Adding audiovisual aids
Providing an outline and any other readings that help to clarify the main points of
  the talk

A commandment that should be followed virtually without exception is: Thou shalt not read your lecture. It would take an actor of consummate skill to keep an audience's attention while reading a text. Relying on notes or an outline is more likely to produce a natural style of delivery and the maintenance of eye contact with the audience.

In using the lecture method, it is essential to stay in touch with the audience. Without frequent feedback, it is very difficult to determine whether the lecture has been effective in conveying information.

The Demonstration

This is probably the most ancient and universal teaching technique. From the beginning of time, human beings have been showing each other how to do the things on which the survival of the individual and the group depends. In adult education, however, the demonstration has been used in a limited way—mainly in vocational education, in the physical sciences, and in such community-related projects as a proposed transportation or waste disposal system.[8] With the growing interest in leisure-time activities, however, the demonstration is being put to good use in the teaching of gourmet cooking, home brewing, macrame, pottery making, and other recreational skills. It is also finding a place in basic education—for example, in showing adults how to use writing instruments and form letters of the alphabet.

The demonstration provides information through simulated or actual operations of tools, machinery, or other equipment. It might be described as an adult version of "Show and Tell" in which the teacher shows the students how certain procedures are performed and what specific tasks and skills are called for while at the same time describing these operations verbally. The main advantage of the demonstration is its usefulness to the teacher in presenting visually the kind of "how to" information that is very difficult to comprehend through aural means alone.

A successful demonstration requires careful preplanning and practice. The teacher must be sure any special equipment to be used is on hand and in good working order and that he or she is thoroughly familiar with its use. In certain instances a demonstration may be enhanced by bringing in outside resources: materials that illuminate a particular procedure or an expert in the performance of the skill being demonstrated.

This technique is not suitable for large classes; the group should be kept to a size where all can have a clear view of the demonstration.

SPECIAL TEACHING ROLES

As a teacher in adult education, you may be called upon from time to time to assume such special roles as guest speaker, moderator, or field study guide. The first is usually in a program taught by another instructor; the second is usually a program for which you have been invited to act as host; the third may take place with either your own or another instructor's class.

The guest speaker is invited to appear at a session of a class, lecture series, or panel program to present authoritative information from his or her field of expertise. Professional programs rely heavily on guest speakers, the arrangements often being on a quid pro quo basis when the guest is also a teacher in the field. Appearing as each other's guests is a fairly common practice among the part-time instructors who are the bulwark of continuing education, and it is an excellent means of enriching and diversifying a class or special program.

When you are invited to do a "guest shot," your first move is to obtain an outline of the course along with any other information that may be relevant to your presentation. If other guest speakers have preceded you, find out what their talks dealt with so that you can avoid redundancy. If it is a panel program, check out what the other panelists will be discussing. A guest speaker is expected to draw upon his or her experience, but without thought and preparation, this can all too easily come across as an "ego trip," particularly if the talk dwells exclusively upon the successful achievements of the guest's professional career. You can counteract this tendency by including an account of your struggles and defeats along the way; there is often as much or more to be learned from an individual's failures as from his or her successes.

Since as a guest speaker, you will be drawing upon familiar material, you may feel that preparation is unnecessary, that you can easily "wing it." Occasionally this may work out, but for the most part it is not advisable. Regardless of how well you know your material, a coherent presentation requires some form of organization—either notes or an outline. The most frequent criticism of guest speakers by adult learners is "rambling and repetitious."

The moderator of a program, whether it is a debate, panel, or lecture series, performs an exacting task that requires poise, quickness, and a high degree of audience sensitivity, as well as knowledge of the subject matter being presented by the speakers. Since the moderating function determines the tone and pace of the presentation, the moderator can often make or break a program.

As a moderator, you and the audience are in a host-guest relationship, and your principal tasks are:

Introduce the panelists or lecturers. You should receive in advance biographies of all those who will be appearing on the program. It is also a good idea to phone each speaker in advance to confirm such logistical details as the time and place of the presentation and the amount of time to be allotted. When introducing speakers, include all information about their training, occupation, and philosophical perspective that may be relevant to the topic.

Draw out the speakers if you feel that they have omitted or minimized certain important aspects of the subject.

In a panel program, develop a dialogue among the panelists and see that no one speaker or point of view dominates the others.

Promote interaction between the speakers and the audience during the question-and-answer session. This will usually work better if you "warm up" the audience first, to give them time to frame questions and comments, lessening the risk of being confronted by an awkward silence when you ask: Any questions?

A few "don'ts" for moderators:

Don't interject your personal opinions. The moderator should at all times maintain a neutral stance.

Don't make personal comments about the speakers on the program.

Don't interrupt a speaker unless he/she runs over the allotted time. When this happens, wait for an appropriate pause in the presentation and then make some tactful reference to time limitations.

Don't take on a moderating assignment when the subject of the program is one in which you have little or no interest or background. You don't have to be an expert in the subject, but you should have sufficient knowledge of what the speakers are discussing so that you can engage intelligently in dialogue with them and pose questions that will stimulate lively interaction.

Don't upstage the speakers. Your effectiveness as a moderator will be enhanced by a low-key manner and a gracious, relaxed style.

Field Study Guide

The growing popularity of study tours has opened up opportunities for instructors to accompany groups of students on field trips that may range all the way from a bus tour of the local botanical gardens to a three-week tour of China. The two principal qualifications for a study tour guide are: (1) You need thorough knowledge of the site to be visited. If the location is a foreign country, you should have a good command of the language and be completely familiar with the subject matter that provides the focus of the trip. (2) You need the ability to relate well to many different kinds of people. On extended trips to foreign countries, you and your students will be together day after day under circumstances that may at time be extremely trying and frustrating. There may be physical discomforts and other inconveniences; tensions and conflicts, flareups of temper in the group, complaints about food and accommodations, and various other problems and crises are likely to arise when people who are strangers to each other are thrown together for a period of time. Patience, tolerance, and humor are the qualities that belong in the survival kit of every field study guide—in fact, are qualities that all teachers of adults might do well to cultivate.

THE TEACHER AS COUNSELOR

Although most medium- to large-size institutions offer special counseling services, the teacher of adults is often seen by students as someone who can offer advice in many of their problem areas. Usually the advice sought will be learning-connected, and here the teacher can often serve a useful function. Teachers have access to information in their areas of study or career fields which can be very valuable to students with specific needs or interests.

A student may ask for a personal appointment to discuss his inability to keep up with the rest of the class. The teacher has an opportunity to analyze and pinpoint the student's difficulty one-to-one. If it becomes evident that inadequate study skills are at the root of the problem, the teacher can steer the student toward a learning skills program and keep a watchful eye for signs of progress. Of if the individual's problem is with the substance of the course, the teacher may wish to assign special readings or other supplementary aids to assist the student in mastering the material.

In career and professional education, the teacher, as a practitioner in the field, is in a position to offer the kind of specialized advice and guidance that are much appreciated by students. An attorney, a public relations practitioner, and an interior designer teaching courses in their respective fields are prime sources for advice on where the jobs are in those fields and how to go about locating them. This is not to suggest that teachers in career and professional fields should serve as full-fledged career counselors; rather, the advice they offer should take the form of fringe benefits and should not replace a comprehensive career guidance program.

THE TEACHER AS PSYCHOLOGICAL COUNSELOR

From time to time, the teacher of adults is thrust inadvertently into the role of psychological counselor. Adult learners lead complicated lives and are often attempting to study under stressful conditions: while undergoing a divorce or caring for an elderly parent or worrying about a sick or troubled child, to cite a few examples. A student may stay after class or ask for a special meeting to discuss a study-related problem and somehow, without either intending it, the meeting turns into another kind of session in which the participants assume a new kind of relationship. A man or woman who up till now has been a member of a class is revealed as a troubled human being in need of a sympathetic ear; the teacher is placed in the position of supplying the sympathy and offering comfort and counsel.

How far should a teacher go in acting as a psychological counselor? This is a risky area, for here, as Gilbert Highet warns, "teaching borders on psychiatry," and he goes on to assert that "in dealing with these cases, there is one sovereign rule. Keep the relationship impersonal. Never step outside the bounds of your profession."[9]

Lending a sympathetic ear is a human reaction, and it is entirely possible to listen with compassion to a student's personal problems while observing Highet's rule. A manual for teachers prepared by UCLA Extension offers some useful guidance on this subject:

> Programs must not be intended as therapy for the participants. While some programs may include a component of counseling, guidance and personal assessment, the distinction between Extension human behavior classes and therapy will be maintained by the absence of any continuing personal obligation between the instructor and the student, by the assumption that the audience is basically healthy and by the avoidance of settings and methods inviting untoward emotional involvement.[10]

When a troubled student seeks help or advice from a teacher regarding problems of a personal nature, the sensible procedure is to refer him or her to the appropriate counseling services. For this reason, it is important for teachers to become acquainted with psychological and other counseling services which may be available both at the institution in which they are teaching and in the larger community.

REFERENCES

1. Robert E. Snyder and Curtis Ulmer, *Guide to Teaching Techniques for Adult Classes,* Prentice-Hall, Englewood Cliffs, N.J., 1972.
2. Leonard Freedman, *Principles of Discussion Leadership,* UCLA Extension, Los Angeles, 1968.
3. Ronald T. Hyman, *Ways of Teaching,* 2nd ed., J. B. Lippincott Co., Philadelphia, 1974.
4. Clark C. Abt, designer of simulation games, in ibid.
5. Ronald Gross, *Higher/Wider/Education,* Ford Foundation Report, New York, 1976.
6. Ibid.
7. B. F. Skinner, The Technology of Teaching, Meredith Corp., 1968, p. 37.
8. Snyder and Ulmer, op. cit.
9. Gilbert Highet, *The Art of Teaching,* Alfred Knopf, New York, 1950.
10. UCLA Extension Standards and Criteria, "Adult Students and Their Problems," Los Angeles, 1979.

Chapter 6

THE SIX-STEP PLANNING PROCESS

Whatever your teaching role, and regardless of the knowledge you bring to your subject, your success as a teacher of adults will depend to a large extent on the planning you put into your teaching. Even a course you have taught many times before requires planning to keep it fresh, updated, and in tune with the varying needs and interests of adult learners. For the creative teacher, no two classes are ever entirely alike and there is always something new to be discovered and applied to future teaching.

Planning a course for adults involves six basic steps:

1. Developing a learner profile
2. Formulating objectives
3. Selecting learning methods
4. Selecting resources
5. Developing a syllabus
6. Evaluating the course

Before you begin the actual planning of your course, a question to consider is, Who are the participants in the process? The principal participants are, of course, you and the learners who will be taking your course. Since learner involvement is a key element in course development, step 6, evaluating, serves as a guide and a correcting device for the planning process. The teacher need not wait, however, until the final evaluation at the conclusion of the course; learners can be involved in the early stages of planning through assessment of their needs and expectations at the first session.

Depending on the teaching situation, others besides the teacher and students involved in the planning process might include the head of the department offering your course; the director of adult education if you are teaching in a high school, academic or other experts, the department head, dean, or similar administrative officer if you are in a college or university setting; and, in a broader sense, the community being served. Institutional policies may also determine the form and content of what you are planning to teach, and acquainting yourself with these at the beginning can be a time and energy saver.

DEVELOPING A LEARNER PROFILE

Who are the adult learners who will be taking your course? What will they bring to the experience? What will they hope to gain? In the elementary grades through college, the teacher has some prior knowledge about the students—at a minimum, their age and previous education. Since adult learners come in all ages and with a broad diversity of education and experience, even this basic information is usually not available to the teacher. With a little research and forethought, you can develop a profile of your potential learners that will give you some sense of direction in designing your course.

You might start by consulting teachers who have taught the same or similar courses before; they can give you a general idea of the age range, occupations, and interests of the people who attended their classes. The department in which you are teaching should be a good source of information and may also be able to provide you with evaluations of past courses designed for learners similar to those your course is aimed at; studying these should offer some idea of what to expect in the way of class composition and expectations.

The way your course is described in the catalog and other promotional materials will also help to define the class you are planning to teach. When the course copy reads, "for teachers, lawyers, ministers, and people who are required to make persuasive presentations" or "for women who function in the multiple roles of career woman, wife, and mother" or "for men and women interested in a law-related career," you have marked off an area within which the potential learners will have several characteristics in common.

The time and location of your course offer further clues. A daytime class will attract a very different group of learners—mainly women who do not work outside the home, the self-employed, and retirees—whereas evening classes include a higher proportion of nine-to-fivers. Locating the class in the central city will alter its composition as compared with a suburban location.

There may be information available in the community which can offer some additional guidance in sketching out a preliminary learner profile. In planning a program for people charged with driving while under the influence of alcohol, the teacher, whose background was in sociology, researched court records to discover the age range, occupations, and proportion of men to women among those cited for the offense of drunken driving. Also, the demography of the community from which the institution offering your course draws its students is a useful source of information in regard to age, income levels, and cultural background.

These strategies are helpful in arriving at a rough estimate of the kind of people for whom you are designing your course. The specifics will be filled in when you meet with your class and assess their needs, interests, and goals.

Needs Assessment

Your plan should include a needs assessment technique that will provide you with as much relevant information as possible about your learners' motivations and expectations. The method in most common use in classes of average size—that is, fifteen to forty students—is the oral introduction: the teacher asks each member of the class to identify himself or herself by name and occupation and state the reason for taking the course. Those who favor this approach claim it helps to warm up the class. Some communications specialists in the field of education maintain that it can have the opposite effect, since it forces a sharing of information before the individuals are ready; this approach can be particularly hard on the more diffident members of the class. An alternative method that works well with large as well as small classes is the written introduction: the class is given a stated time interval at the beginning of the session in which to provide the requested information. The written introduction gives the teacher an opportunity to study the learners' self-assessments and use them as a basis for refining the initial plan. Instead of going through a formal introduction at the first meeting, the learners become acquainted with each other gradually through their informal interaction and their participation in the work of the class.

FORMULATING OBJECTIVES

How do you determine the objectives for the course you are planning to teach? In traditional education, the teacher decides, within the structure of the institutional curriculum, what is to be taught and how it is to be taught within specified time limits. The students must then conform to these standards if they wish to receive a passing grade in the course.

There are many areas of adult education in which this reactive approach is entirely appropriate—language instruction, for example. Suppose you are teaching Intermediate Spanish. The prerequisite is Elementary Spanish, and the course that follows is advanced Spanish, so you have a fairly clear idea of where your instruction should begin and leave off. This approach would apply to many credit courses, regardless of the subject matter, in which there are upper and lower content boundaries.

The emphasis in recent years on specific, measurable objectives grew out of the dissatisfaction of educators with what they perceived as the vague, unscientific nature of the teaching profession, which had made it difficult for teachers to be held accountable. Objectives measurable in terms of behavioral change have been hailed as the solution and have, in fact, been helpful in providing teachers and learners with a sense of direction.

The essential component of the behavioral objective is a statement setting forth what the learner will achieve in ability to perform or in attitudinal change. The statement also specifies the conditions under which the behavioral change will take place, the criteria for the change, and the time limit. For a class in English as a Second Language, a behavioral objective might specify: At the end of four weeks, the learner will be able to use correctly 100 English words in simple declarative sentences. A test given at the end of the four-week period will demonstrate how closely the objective has been achieved.

Behavioral objectives have several advantages: they help define purpose and method for the teacher, they give the learners a clear idea of what is expected of them, they serve as a useful tool in developing tests and evaluation criteria, they provide learners with a yardstick for measuring their progress, and they are invaluable in preparing learners to meet job or educational standards, for example, civil service exams or the high school equivalency test. Since objectives that measure learner performance are teacher-centered, they cannot be rigidly applied to the expanding noncredit field in such areas as personal or career development. Here there are usually no prerequisites or predetermined standards and often no neat, readymade packages of learning materials. The boundaries are flexible or nonexistent, and the learning that takes place depends as much on the learners as on the instructor. It is one thing to formulate objectives for a course in Analytic Geometry, open only to those who have taken Mathematics 3A, and something else to determine precisely what is to be learned in Self-Perception and Misperception or Assertiveness Training or The Art of Fund Raising. In courses like these, learners bring with them their wide diversity of needs, goals, and experience, resources the teacher draws upon in developing objectives.

Arriving at objectives through a teacher-learner partnership opposes the basic assumption of the behavioral objectives approach, that there is a body of knowledge external to the individual which can be acquired through standardized methods. In educational theory, this is a highly debatable proposition and one that has been argued exhaustively since the dawn of philosophy. At a practical level, teachers of adults are confronted by certain functional realities that challenge the fixed-body-of-external-knowledge theory and call upon their ability to adapt and modify. As Jerold Apps has observed: Once a learning activity begins, it may become obvious that the focus of the activity should be changed and the objectives modified. Indeed the learners may demand that a change be made. This may mean abandoning some previously determined objectives, modifying others, or adding new ones. If the teacher has to adhere to a pre-planned set of behavioral objectives, these options are impossible."[1]

This does not mean that the teacher should abandon the procedure of including objectives in the course plan. The key to all preplanning is openness. Suppose the course to be taught is Creative Writing. The teacher who, let us say, is interested primarily in the novel, has an objective: that each member of the class will, by midpoint, have developed a detailed outline and written a chapter of a novel. When the class assembles, the needs assessment reveals that most learners are not interested in writing novels; they are seeking guidance in writing non-fiction articles and short stories. The teacher's original objective is not very useful under these circumstances and must be modified to meet the goals of the learners.

In this case, the question that suggests itself is, Why start out with an objective at all? There are critics of behavioral objectives who would answer the question by asserting that there is no point in framing objectives in advance, that it is presumptuous for the teacher to impose his or her purposes on learners without their active participation in the process. The assumption here is that the teacher's role is not only equivalent to but identical with that of the learners, that all are engaged equally in an open-ended dialogue.

This approach is associated with the educational philosophy of Paulo Freier a South American educator who emphasizes the social context in which learning takes place. The Freirian scheme views education as a search in which people discover the social realities of their world, the discovery emerging out of dialogue and involvement by all in the group. According to Freire, education is never neutral; it is either a liberating or an oppressive force in people's lives. Even those fields of study generally considered value-free, such as physics or linguistics, when detached from the social fabric become sterile techniques. Education should be holistic, and through the dialectical process, should raise the consciousness of the group toward the ultimate aim of social change growing out of individual change.

Freire regards traditional education as a form of "banking" in which knowledge is something to be distributed. He describes it as "an act of depositing, in which the students are the depositories and the teacher is the depositor. Instead of communicating, the teacher issues communiques and makes deposits which the students patiently receive, memorize and repeat . . . the scope of the action allowed to the students extends only as far as receiving, filing and storing deposits."[2]

The Freirian approach poses a dilemma for the American educational system, which is based on a very different set of cultural imperatives. Even ardent pro-

Freirians have expressed doubts about the compatibility of this humanistic view of learning with the American emphasis on efficiency, structure, and goals in education. Also, the insistence on education as a process of social change leads, as some critics have commented, to conflict and polarization.[3]

For Freire, the teacher is a coordinator who, like the facilitator or discussion leader, merely helps move things along, but in the American system of education —and here the traditional and nontraditional modes have something in common —it is generally accepted that the teacher has something specific to offer, something from which the learners hope to benefit. This does not mean that the teacher must act as an authority figure, in Freire's term, a "banker" issuing knowledge to the learner-"depositors." It simply requires that the teacher take the initiative in developing a flexible structure and purpose for the class and be prepared to adapt and modify that structure and purpose as required by the individuals in the class.

SELECTING LEARNING METHODS

Commitment to a particular technique or to a narrow range of methods is incompatible with the creative approach to teaching. The teacher of adults, as we've seen, has a wealth of methods available for accomplishing the purpose of the course. The decision as to which should be selected is determined by such intrinsic factors as the learning objectives as well as by such extrinsic factors as class size and available time, space, and facilities.

As with many other creative enterprises, in teaching form is inseparable from content. The underlying question is, How can I, as a teacher, present what I have to offer so that it is of maximum benefit to the learners? Putting the question this way implies a merging of process and content, a recognition of the fact that "the critical content of any learning experience is the method or process through which the learning occurs."[4] Hearing a Greek temple described in a lecture, seeing it on television, or viewing the actual structure during a field study trip to Greece will produce very different experiences for the learner. The attempt to separate content from process in education has set up a false dichotomy that is antithetical to the pursuit of wholeness in continuing education.

Having sketched out one or more flexible learning objectives, the logical next step is to analyze what the course has to offer: Is it mainly information or mainly skills or a combination of the two? Is the emphasis on the cognitive or the affective realm of learning, or are mastery of knowledge and change of attitude given equal weight? How much time is required to accomplish these goals? Depending upon the answers that result from your analysis, you may decide on several techniques to carry out the purpose of the course, for example, a blend of lecture, discussion, role playing, and independent study.

As with the development of objectives, you should be prepared to make modifications or substitutions in the methods you select as required by the exigencies of the actual teaching situation. Unless it is possible to predict class size with some degree of accuracy, your decisions regarding methodology will have to be "soft." You can often vary your techniques without drastic alterations in the original plan: Your course may be intended for a maximum of thirty learners and is designed as a seminar or workshop with a heavy emphasis on individual participation. The actual class size, however, turns out to be double or triple what you had anticipated. You have the option of dividing the class into sections and teaching them at different times or, if this is not feasible, arranging the students in subgroups and monitoring their progress with the assistance of group leaders.

The Time Element

In much of adult education, the time frame for your course is your decision, and you may find yourself confronted with what appear to be a bewildering array of choices. Should it be a one-day program? A weekend? A short course (four meetings)? A one-week intensive course? An eight-week lecture discussion series? A sixteen-day field study tour? The choice of a time period is determined by breaking down the overall plan into units or modules and assigning to each the time required, according to your best estimate.

If you have never taught this or a similar course before, you may have to do some educated guessing. After arriving at what you regard as a suitable time frame for the purpose of the course, you still have to consider the other half of the equation: the learners for whom the course is intended. Is it a professional audience who might prefer an intensive weekend conference in place of an extended once-a-week format? Is it a general-interest audience, more attuned to meeting on a regular basis over a span of time? What about their income level in relation to course fees? Would a short course at a lower fee be more feasible than a longer course at a proportionately higher fee? These are the kinds of questions that enter into your choice of a time period and that are basic to the development of your plan.

The Place

The diversity of locations available for adult learning is suggested in Chapter 1; however, much of the actual learning activity in continuing education, particularly that which takes place in traditional secondary and postsecondary institutions, is located in classrooms reminiscent to most adults of those in which they spend their early schooling years. Of these traditional classrooms, the ones with the fixed rows of seats are the most inappropriate for adult learning. Designed for an educational system in which passive students sit in rigid postures and listen to the teacher, the tendency, when an adult class meets in such a room, is to reinforce passivity. As a result, the teacher has to make an extra effort to counteract the physical setup.

Whenever possible, the teacher should inspect in advance the room in which the class is scheduled to meet. A checklist for a suitable classroom should include:

Size. Is the room too large? Too small? A large room or auditorium sparsely filled discourages interaction. A jam-packed room generates feelings of discomfort and increases distractions.

Seating arrangement. Can seats be arranged in accordance with the plan for the course: small groups, seminar, workshop? If work surfaces are required, are there tables available?

Ventilation. Are there windows that can be opened? Can the room be kept at a comfortable temperature, regardless of seasonal weather conditions?

Acoustics. Can students in the back of the room hear as well as those in the front? Are microphones necessary? If it is a large auditorium, will there be standup microphones for questions and comments by the audience?

Facilities. Is there a blackboard? A flip chart? A screen for audiovisual presentations? A lectern? A table and chairs if there are to be several panelists? (If the program is designed as a dialogue involving two or more speakers, a living room arrangement with comfortable chairs is preferable to the usual stiff hardback seats that are placed on platforms.)

Convenience. If the program provides for coffee breaks and/or lunch, is there a place nearby where these provisions can be obtained?

Where the teacher is free to select the setting for a continuing education activity, imagination together with a sense of the appropriate can lead to a choice of location that adds an important dimension to the learning experience. A program on local history, for example, might be held in one or more of the existing historical sites: a fort or mission or a museum with a relevant collection. A class on radio production belongs, for all practical purposes, in a broadcasting studio, a theater history class in a theater, a drawing class in a studio. The New School conducts classes in fashion design and merchandising in New York's garment district.[5]

Residential programs, many of which are professional conferences, are customarily held in hotels, in which case the instructor or coordinator should investigate in advance the available space and facilities, using the suggested checklist as a guide.

SELECTING RESOURCES

In continuing education, learning resources are so vast and varied they offer the teacher an "embarrassment of riches." According to one definition, learning resources are "those items and individuals which present the stimuli needed for most learning to occur."[6] It would be impossible to develop a complete compendium of resources for adult learning since these are constantly expanding, but the teacher should be aware of at least the following categories: written materials, commercially and teacher-prepared; films, filmstrips, slides, audiotapes, videotapes; photos, charts, and other materials to be used with an overhead projector; guest speakers; performances (dramatic vignettes and playlets); role playing and simulating-gaming materials; programmed materials; exercises; self-analysis aids.

Resources should be selected for the sole purpose of advancing the objectives of the course and should add a specific and relevant learning dimension. They should not be utilized, as they too often are, for cosmetic purposes or as a crutch for the teacher: for example, films should not be presented merely because they are entertaining and will, the teacher hopes, liven up the class, or because the teacher has nothing else with which to fill that portion of the class time.

A few guidelines for selecting and using learning resources:

All learning resources should be checked out in advance. Written materials should be reviewed and audiovisual materials previewed.

Resources should be an integral part of the overall plan and not simply tacked on as an afterthought.

Audiovisual presentations usually require the support of reading materials such as study guides.

Resources should be appropriate to the learners' skill levels; for example, in basic education and English as a Second Language, materials should not be so advanced as to discourage the learners.

The use of programmed materials requires constant monitoring by the teacher to determine where learners are encountering difficulty and to reinforce their progress.

Learners should be given adequate preparation for the introduction of learning resources so that they have a clear comprehension of how the resource fits into the educational plan.

Guest speakers should be thoroughly briefed as to what is expected of them; they should also have a clear idea of their position in the learning sequence so that they do not repeat material that has already been covered or that is to be dealt with by a guest speaker scheduled for a future date.

The selection of learning resources may be limited by such budgetary constraints as renting films or reproducing written materials or paying guest speakers, and these considerations must enter into the planning. The imaginative teacher, however, will discover that by canvassing the community a cornucopia of resources can be obtained without cost from local organizations, business and industry, professional groups, and others who are interested in providing materials for educational purposes. There is another excellent resource that should not be overlooked: the learners themselves. The teacher who is skillful in drawing out the members of the class will uncover a rich reservoir of information and experience that is often directly related to the content of the course and that offers insights not available elsewhere.

DEVELOPING A SYLLABUS

The outline or syllabus of your course is the culmination of the thinking and planning that has gone before. The syllabus is the blueprint for the teaching-learning transaction that will take place and therefore deserves to be carefully thought out and developed. Like the other components of your plan, however, the structure it projects should not be cast in concrete but should have an open plan and movable walls.

Since you will be handing out the syllabus to the learners at the first session, it should provide them with a clear and concise view of the plan for the course and what is expected of them. In addition to specifying what will be taking place in each of the time segments, it should also include a list of readings, required or recommended; assignments; testing dates; and any scheduled films, guest speakers, field trips, or other special events. Though not strictly necessary, it is also helpful to append brief biographies of scheduled guest speakers and any other supplementary materials, such as maps, charts, diagrams, and statistics that might highlight the course content. (See the Syllabus Model, Table 6.1.)

How closely the course will adhere to the syllabus depends largely on whether you are teaching mainly in the proactive or the reactive mode. In the more traditional format, the syllabus usually predicts with a high degree of specificity the activities that will take place in the classroom. In nontraditional approaches, particularly in noncredit learning, the syllabus tends to serve rather as a flexible guide and may go through several changes during the course of the actual learning experience. Whatever the teaching style or situation, the creative teacher is constantly reality-testing and striving to bring his/her instructional plans and purposes into harmony with the learners' goals and capabilities.

Testing and Grading

For many adults, the most unpleasant memories of their previous schooling are associated with taking examinations and receiving grades. This was a punitive

TABLE 6.1. A Syllabus Model

COURSE PLAN
1. Course objectives
2. Topics planned for each session

RESOURCES
1. Guest speakers with biographies
2. Schedule of audiovisual presentations
3. Supplementary materials such as charts, diagrams, statistics

REQUIREMENTS
1. Learner participation
2. Required and/or recommended reading list
3. Assignments
4. Field trips (dates and sites)
5. Examination dates

process that struck fear into the heart of the student and made learning into a contest that one either won or lost. In ascribing this system of testing and grading to male-imposed standards, John McLeish has observed that, in measuring students against predetermined standards, "the student was gleefully tested for weakness, and if enough weaknesses were detected, it was decided that he was not entitled to the right to further learning. Testing also rated students on a scale, following the status principle that belonged to slavery. What mattered was not how good a student was but how much better he was than his fellows."[7]

In adult education, tests should be an integral part of the learning process. They should be learner-centered, designed to assist learners in keeping track of their progress. The emphasis should be not on memorizing and regurgitating but on thinking and discovering. As active participants in their education, adults can be involved in the development of their own individualized examinations as well as in self-grading. According to one grading method, learners are asked, in a written assignment, to suggest a grade for themselves and give their reasons. If the teacher does not agree with a learner's self-assigned grade, the difference can be discussed and negotiated until both parties agree on a grade that accurately reflects the learner's progress.

Standard approaches to testing and grading have come in for sharp criticism in recent years and, in continuing education, there are signs of a growing preference for substituting research papers or other learning-related projects as a basis for assigning grades. The resourceful teacher who is genuinely committed to the learning process will find any number of ways to help that process along in a positive, encouraging, and nonpunitive manner.

EVALUATING: THE TEACHER'S FEEDBACK LOOP

Evaluation, properly used and applied, can serve as the teacher's most important planning tool. Not until the evaluations are in can the teacher have anything approaching an objective view of the learning that took place and the extent to which the planning done for the course was realized. As a planning tool, however, evaluation is a two-edged sword: on the one side, it shears away any illusions or misperceptions that teachers may have been harboring in regard to their performance; on the other, the information that is gleaned may distort what took place in the class and thus give teachers a false idea of how their performance and planning actually worked.

Evaluation methods commonly used in adult education are:

The survey instrument or questionnaire, either standardized or developed for an individual class or program. In the larger continuing education institutions, the introduction of computerization has virtually mandated the use of standardized forms.

Telephone interviews; these usually play a limited role, mainly as a follow-up to written questionnaires.

Unobtrusive measures; these consist mainly of reports based on observation by administrative staff and/or professional evaluators on the number of participants, the age range, the proportion of men to women, the degree of participation, etc.

Subjective measures; these include hunches, commonsense reactions, analyses based on previous experience with similar learning situations, and off-the-cuff judgments in regard to learning satisfaction.

The usual procedure is for learners to be given a set of questionnaires to be filled out anonymously at the last session of the course or during the last hour of a one-day or weekend program. The questionnaires are collected and analyzed—and here there is considerable variation, depending upon institutional size and policies. In a large extension operation, evaluations are usually studied by the program staff before the results are passed on to the teachers. In smaller organizations, teachers may be solely responsible for collecting and analyzing evaluations (see simple evaluation forms, Appendixes C and D).

Whatever the evaluation methods or procedures, it is the teacher who is finally confronted as the party of the first part by what the learners have to say about their recent experience in his or her class. At this point judgment, perspicacity, and the ability to put one's ego aside are necessary in order to interpret the evaluations constructively. The key questions that provide a framework for such an interpretation are:

Do the results indicate a generally thoughtful response to the questions—or do they seem to come "off the top of the head" of a substantial proportion of the responders?

Are the results contradictory—and if so, how can the contradictions be resolved?
Is there a common thread running through the response which suggests either that
  the course is on the right track or that improvement is needed?

In regard to the first question, the thoughtfulness of the responses can usually
be gauged by the learners' written comments in the space provided for this
purpose on most evaluation forms. These comments are likely to be the most
revealing section of the evaluation, and therefore the questionnaire should provide ample space for these comments and learners should be given sufficient time
to set down their thoughts in writing. If the standardized forms do not allow for
adequate space for learners' comments, the teacher should provide a supplementary form to make up for this deficiency.

The problem of contradictory evaluation results is a tricky one. What is the
teacher to make of it when several responses characterize the class as "boring,
repetitious, a waste of time," while several others state, "most interesting and
valuable class I've ever taken"? The teacher may conclude that the truth lies
somewhere in between or—as is very often the case—that, because of the wide
range of skills and experience among adult learners, both sets of responses are
true.

The missing link in the usual evaluation procedure, which is responsible for
much of its ambiguity, is the learner as a participant in the experience. Evaluation
designs in adult education are generally reactive rather than proactive: They do
not take into consideration the moods, emotions, personal problems, or other
subjective states of the responder during the teaching-learning activity. There is
no provision for self-analysis, for an attempt on the part of the individuals in the
class to relate their performance to the final result. Nor is there any allowance
for the learners' feelings toward the teacher, which can influence their responses
to a considerable extent.

There is also the possibility of distortion through what is known as the "Dr.
Fox syndrome." This refers to an educational experiment at a medical school in
which an actor was introduced to a group of professional practitioners as Dr. Fox,
a distinguished expert in their subject area. Actually he knew nothing at all about
the subject, but, having been carefully coached, he presented in a lively and
humorous manner a lecture that had very little to do with the topic. Not only
did the participants rate him as a highly effective teacher, but they also claimed
they had learned much from the presentation which they would be able to make
use of in their work. Moral: Charisma can often compensate for lack of substance.

Professional evaluators are doubtful that providing an opportunity for self-
analysis on questionnaires would yield useful information. They maintain that
such an analysis would require a greater degree of self-knowledge and objectivity
that can be expected from most individuals. It remains up to the teacher to

TABLE 6.2.   Checklist of Instructor Tasks Prior to Start of Class

_____ 1. Select and order textbooks and other course materials.

_____ 2. Identify potential proctors.

_____ 3. Select course assistant.

_____ 4. Interview and select proctor staff.

_____ 5. Develop course calendar.

    _____ a. Determine number of class days in quarter, excluding holidays.

    _____ b. Determine the number of course study units.

    _____ c. Determine the *minimum* number of testing days required (a general rule is to multiply the number of units by 8/5).

    _____ d. Schedule films.

    _____ e. Schedule guest lectures.

    _____ f. Schedule other special events (field trips, etc.).

    _____ g. Schedule demonstration apparatus and order any necessary supplies for demonstrations.

    _____ h. Schedule other essential lectures.

_____ 6. Distribute proctor manual to proctors.

_____ 7. Examine classroom to see if it is appropriate for essential classroom activities.

supply the missing link as part of his or her interpretation of evaluation results. In most cases, when most of the responses agree on a characterization of the class, either negative or positive, the teacher can assume the statements are reasonably accurate. These data then serve as the feedback loop, the final stage of the planning process, which is also the key to more effective, better-informed planning in the future.

REFERENCES

1. Jerold W. Apps, *Toward a Working Philosophy of Adult Education,* Publications in Continuing Education, Syracuse University, Syracuse, N.Y., 1973.
2. Paulo Freire, *Pedagogy of the Oppressed,* Herder and Herder, New York, 1971, p. 58.

3. William S. Griffith, "Paulo Freire: Utopian Perspective on Literacy Education for Revolution," in Stanley M. Grabowski, ed., *Paulo Freire: A Revolutionary Dilemma for the Adult Educator,* ERIC Clearinghouse on Adult Education, Syracuse, N.Y., 1972.

4. Neil Postman and Charles Weingartner, *Teaching as a Subversive Activity,* Dell, New York, 1969.

5. Elinor Lenz, *Creating and Marketing Programs in Continuing Education,* McGraw-Hill, New York, 1980, p. 80.

6. Robert E. Snyder and Curtis Ulmer, *Guide to Teaching Techniques for Adult Classes,* Prentice-Hall, Englewood Cliffs, N.J., 1972, p. 28.

7. Ibid., p. 48.

Chapter 7

A CATALOG OF COMMON TEACHING FAULTS AND HOW TO OVERCOME THEM

One of the sacred tenets of traditional education is that learning automatically follows teaching. If the teacher has been engaged in the activity of teaching and the students are not learning, it is clearly the "fault" of the students. They, the students, are graded, and they either "pass" or "fail." The teacher is not graded; the teacher always "passes," even if every student in the class "fails."

When the respect for authority that sustained this creed was shaken up by the protests of the sixties, doctors, police, and the educational establishment were brought down from their pedestals and subjected to sharp scrutiny and criticism by the lay public. In education, this change in the public consciousness has had a continuing impact on teachers from elementary through postsecondary levels, and while the concept of malpractice has not yet found its way into education, as it has in medicine, there is a growing sense that teachers must share responsibility for the miseducation as well as the education of their students. Behavioral objectives and sophisticated methods of teacher evaluation have been developed in the hope that they would provide tools for measuring teacher performance and holding teachers accountable.

In continuing education, the idea of shared responsibility is reinforced by the partnership between teacher and learner. The learner must be actively involved in the educational process, but the teacher, as facilitator or discussion leader or whatever the role, can either help or hinder that process. It is important, therefore, that the teacher of adults be aware of faults that can impede the learner's

70

progress and reduce the effectiveness of the best-laid plans and preparation. The following catalog of teaching faults are those that occur most frequently, according to learner evaluations.

WASTING TIME

Adults bring to learning a sense of time very different from that of younger students. In much of adult education, learners are paying their own way, and time equals money. Even when their education is being subsidized, the time that adults can invest in learning is usually borrowed from other pursuits and must be shoehorned in somehow among the many demands and pressures of adult life.

"Too much time was wasted," is a comment that appears at the top of the list of learner complaints. Time-wasting can take many forms. There is the teacher who consistently arrives late for the start of class, a practice guaranteed to raise the irritation level of the waiting learners, who have hurried away from work or rushed through dinner or are paying a sitter so they could attend the class. Other familiar time-wasters are scheduling frequent, too-lengthy coffee breaks; extending the lunch hour (in one-day programs); dismissing the class earlier than called for in the schedule. Treating learning time in this cavalier way leads the members of the class to suspect, usually with some justification, not only that the teacher has no respect for their time but also that he or she has planned poorly and is not prepared to fill the allotted time. A negative image is set up of the teacher as a model for skillful time management, which is so important for the adult learner. Additional time-eroders include dawdling; dwelling on irrelevancies; rambling; repeating; fussing with defective audivisual equipment that was not checked out in advance; using anecdotes, jokes, and other extraneous material as time-fillers.

The reaction of adults to such abuse of their time is expressed in the following excerpts from a learner's letter of complaint:

> He [a public relations consultant teaching a class on the basics of public relations] has wasted my time and money on irrelevant word games and stories and has not used the class time for the teaching of public relations. . . . We have heard a tape of a television comedy sketch having nothing to do with public relations, followed by a half hour reading of cute aphorisms written by someone else. . . . Out of eighteen hours of class time one hour has been devoted to our ten-week project, the term paper. . . . He dwells on his own professional experience, which is far ahead of an introductory class like this one. . . . A story now and then is fine but the same ones over and over create a strange combination of monotony and rage. It seems to me that he is ignoring his responsibility as a teacher and is more concerned with what he finds to be entertaining.

Respect for learners' time should be an integral part of the teacher's attitude. A few simple rules can help in overcoming time-wasting practices:

Always meet the class on time and hold fast to the time scheduled for breaks.
Resist the temptation to be entertaining at the expense of what the learners hope to gain from the course.
Plan each session so that you are sure all the time will be used productively. It is better to be over- than underprepared.

PATRONIZING AND TALKING DOWN

Teachers are often unaware of the tone and manner they adopt in class and are surprised when they are described in the evaluations as "patronizing and talking down." This fault occurs among both professional and nonprofessional teachers but is more likely to be found among those who have taught in traditional systems. When teachers are accustomed to regarding themselves as custodians of a body of knowledge that is being proffered to passive receivers, it may be difficult for them to approach adult learners as peers. Since adults are sensitively attuned to this type of treatment, the talking-down approach sets up barriers between teacher and learners that frustrate the teaching-learning relationship.

Status Signals, Verbal and Nonverbal

The patronizing tone comes through in various ways, but essentially it expresses a sense of the teacher's superior status vis-à-vis the learners. This can be communicated both verbally and nonverbally. An obvious verbal cue is the use of names: the teacher refers to the members of the class by first names while they use the formal last name mode of address. Less obvious but equally effective in verbally conveying a higher-status–lower-status relationship are these:

Making personal comments, intended to be flattering, usually by male teachers to female learners, examples: "That's a very attractive outfit you're wearing"; "I like your new hairstyle."
Assuming that all members of the class are at an equal level of ignorance: defining familiar terms, overexplaining, oversimplifying
Showing little interest in learners' ideas or opinions
Directing and controlling learning activities

Nonverbal cues convey status signals as loudly and clearly as the verbal kind. Research in nonverbal communication demonstrates that messages are constantly being sent through eye contact, posture, and gestures. According to a study by British researchers, "it is within the prerogatives of the more powerful to tell others where and how to look and not look; that is, the higher-status person can control the gaze of the lower-status one. Officers can order soldiers to keep their eyes straight ahead; teachers can tell students to give visual attention when being spoken to."[1] The teacher who remains seated behind a desk or stands behind a lectern or on a raised platform; maintains a relaxed position in contrast to an upright posture by members of the class; uses condescending gestures, such as a pat on the head or the shoulder, makes adult learners feel they are being placed in a subordinate position.

EGO-TRIPPING

For the teacher who is on an ego trip, the classroom is a minitheater, the learners a captive audience, the theme of the drama "Teacher Knows Best," and the teacher, of course, performing the solo starring role. The ego-tripping teacher usually prefers the lecture method, which trains the spotlight on the star performer and keeps the learners in their role as the appreciative audience (or so the teacher assumes). Driven by the desire to occupy center stage at all times, the teacher on an ego trip can be identified by the following behaviors:

Constantly uses the pronoun "I"
Draws heavily upon personal experience in offering examples of successful achievements; relies too much on "here's my background, what are your questions?"
Places own book or other writings on required reading list even when not directly relevant to the substance of the class
Refuses to be upstaged
Interrupts frequently during guest speakers' presentations
Makes little or no effort to get feedback from learners

A starting point for overcoming ego-tripping is a heightened sense of self-awareness. Like the patronizer, the ego-tripper is often unaware of how he or she is being perceived by the learners. A strategy that sometimes works is audiotaping, or better still, videotaping, a few classes. When the tapes are played back and analyzed, teachers can develop an objective view of their self-projection in the classroom. Hearing and seeing themselves as they are heard and seen by the learner often provides the salutary shock that is the beginning of a change in teaching style.

PROPAGANDIZING

Teachers, like other people, are valuing beings with ideas and opinions of their own, and it is unrealistic to expect that these personal values and points of view can be kept out of the classroom. Nor is there any reason why the teacher should maintain a strictly neutral stance at all times. There is, though, a crucial difference between sharing a viewpoint and imposing it. The first represents an interchange between mutually respectful individuals; the second is propagandizing, which in some of its more extreme forms, in and out of the classroom, amounts to what has come to be known as brainwashing.

To "propagandize," according to Webster, is to "spread a particular doctrine or system of doctrines or principles." This is the very antithesis of education, which is, by definition, a "drawing out," and which seeks to present a many-faceted view of a subject, the essence of learning being the ability to make intelligent choices.

The teacher as an authority figure has an advantage in this respect over students who are conditioned to accept what they receive in the classroom as the gospel truth. In the reactive setting, the teacher can subtly or openly influence students toward a particular "doctrine or system of doctrines or principles." The potential for such influence is, of course, greater in the social sciences and liberal arts than in mathematics or the physical sciences, and it is this perception that is behind the attempt in recent years to emulate scientific methods in such disciplines as history, social sciences, and even literature.

Whatever the subject being taught, it is the teacher's responsibility to present a balanced view and avoid any suggestion that there is only one acceptable perspective. When a guest speaker is invited who presents a particular position, another guest speaker should be brought in to offer a varying approach to the topic. In assigning readings, the teacher should be sure that the books and articles on the reading list reflect a diversity of viewpoints. At times it may be necessary for the teacher to act as devil's advocate in order to present views that have not been expressed.

In proactive teaching, propagandizing is less likely to be a problem, but the tendency to push one's own views and values can be insidious and is something the teacher should be on guard against in all teaching roles and situations.

"WINGING IT"

Many teachers of adults, particularly in career and vocational areas, have little or no formal training in what they are teaching. Most of what they know has been learned through experience, and this accumulated experience is what they have to offer to the learners who come to their classes. Since their own learning has been acquired in an unstructured manner, they often harbor the mistaken belief that no structure is required in passing on what they have learned. They feel they know the subject so thoroughly, are living with it so closely day by day, that there is no reason to spend time on preparation; instead, they are convinced, they can "wing it," drawing upon their hard-won knowledge and relying on their mental agility to fill the class time.

This ad hoc attitude appears more often among guest speakers and moderators than among regular instructors. Wherever and whenever it appears, it invariably has a negative effect on the learners, who become aware of it very quickly. Typical complaints are "incoherent" "no goals" "no syllabus" "no continuity" "too fragmented" "not clear enough about what was wanted."

It is a fallacy to assume that being steeped in a subject assures that it can be effectively communicated from "the top of one's head." In practicing any creative endeavor, a thorough knowledge of the material is only as valuable as the ability to make it come alive for others. Similarly, the teacher must invest time and thought in preparation if the substance of the course is to take on shape and meaning for the learners.

There is a further fallacy in the assumption that, because the structure for adult learning is often loose, advance planning is not necessary. In fact, the flexible plan that works best in much adult learning involves more forethought than the rigid plan. Providing for flexibility and responding to learners' needs requires ongoing planning and monitoring so that the teacher-learning activity can maintain its freshness and dynamism.

OVERLOADING

A question that has particular application to the teaching of adults is: How much is too much? How do you know when you're overloading learners, giving them more than they can handle? Conversely, how can you tell when you're demanding too little to keep them interested and challenged?

There is a delicate balance between too much and too little at all levels of education, but particularly when the learners are working adults saddled with many obligations and responsibilities. Despite the high degree of motivation and commitment that adults bring to learning, there are limits on time and energy that put a brake on how much the learner can accomplish outside of class.

In high school and college, the time in class often represents a small proportion of the total time that is spent meeting the requirements of the course. Two or more hours for every hour of class time is not considered excessive for students who are studying full time. In most cases these extra-classroom activities are, in fact, the most important component of the learning process. Adult education, in which most learners are studying part time, calls for a more realistic proportioning of time spent in and out of class. The teacher's plan should place as much emphasis as possible on learning tasks and activities that can be performed during class time. In assigning work to be done outside of class, the constraints on the learners' time and energy should be taken into consideration. One of the causes of dropping out among adult learners is their discouragement when they find they cannot handle the workload of the course.

Evaluations of a journalism course that was generally faulted for "the rigorous assignments given with no preparatory information" yielded these suggestions for avoiding the fault of overloading:

> Shorten writing assignments.
> Detail specific writing assignments on the syllabus that is distributed the first session
>   so learners will know what is expected and can plan accordingly.
> Perform more assignments in class.

Teachers who have been successful in achieving a balanced workload attribute it to careful listening and observation. Says one instructor in vocational education, "I can pick up a lot of information about my students and what their personal lives are like by paying attention to what they say and how they handle themselves in class." Paying attention and responding to cues from learners are the teacher's most reliable guides in steering a course between too little and too much.

MUDDLING THROUGH

The terms "rambling" and "repetitious" turn up frequently in teacher evaluations. This fault is usually due to poor preparation and is an almost invariable by-product of "winging it." Teachers or guest speakers who muddle through are often highly imaginative, with a rich store of ideas and information to share with their students. In many cases, it is their very creativity and their well-stocked minds that lead them astray in communicating with the class. They toss out an array of glittering insights without developing any of them in depth, interrupt themselves, repeat themselves, take frequent sidetracks, and move from one subject to another without providing transitions.

Muddlers as a rule are fond of the anecdotal style and the phrase "that reminds me of" that punctuates their presentations and acts as a warning flag, signaling to learners that they are about to be taken off the track again. The muddling manner also tends to deflect learners' questions: the question is rarely answered directly but instead triggers still another tangential line of thought.

This type of disjointed delivery can be counted on to leave the audience in a state of confusion. Even when they have been treated to a dazzling display of verbal pyrotechnics, they remain with a sense of having been denied the nourishment they were expecting, as if they had been fed a meal consisting entirely of desserts.

The remedies for muddling through are planning and consistency. A well-thought-out syllabus or outline will help the teacher or guest speaker avoid rambling and hopping from one subject to another. A good plan promotes consistency, which provides a sense of direction and helps learners move toward their goals in a logical and coherent manner.

DISTANCING

As an authority figure, the teacher is automatically set off from the students. In elementary and secondary levels, the age difference between students and teacher adds to the separation between the two. In college, where some of the younger professors are not much older than their students, the distance is preserved by the advanced degrees and scholarly accomplishments of the faculty.

In adult education, these distancing factors are either absent or have assumed a somewhat different form. Teachers of adults may be the same age as or younger than the learners in their classes. Though they may have advanced degrees and a string of scholarly accomplishments to their credit, this does not necessarily set them off from adults whose life experiences—as workers, parents, consumers— entitle them to be treated as equals.

The teacher who adopts a highly formal manner in order to maintain what he or she regards as a proper distance from the learners runs the risk of appearing cold and uncaring. This does not suggest a move to the opposite extreme, where the teacher becomes a pal and conducts the class in an atomosphere of relentless good-buddyship. The proper distance between teachers and adult learners can be compared to that of leader and group seeking common goals in various types of enterprises. Examples are supervisor and work force, director and acting troupe, sales manager and sales staff. As in these related relationships, the teacher-learner connection should contain elements of attachment and detachment. A recent analysis of what makes for good teaching sums it up neatly: "The relationship between students and teacher is emotional as well as intellectual. The social relationship can remain warm and close; the intellectual one should remain somewhat detached."[2]

FAILING TO GET FEEDBACK FROM LEARNERS

The teacher who believes that learning automatically follows teaching tends to communicate with learners unilaterally. There are elements of ego-tripping in this style, which is also characterized by some or all of the following:

Favors the lecture mode

Rarely asks for questions or comments

Assumes that if students are awake and taking notes, they must be learning something

When work is assigned in class or as homework, often fails to collect it

Views students as a collective entity, "the class," rather than as disparate and differing individuals

Believes learning is give-and-take, with the teacher giving and students taking

Places responsibility for failure to learn entirely on students

Gives only one exam—a final—or at most a midterm and final, or, alternately, assigns one term paper

Is a careful planner and preparer, but since all counteracting information is shut out, never deviates from the plan

These practices occur most often among academicians who are trained as researchers rather than as teachers and who, when they take on an assignment in adult education, automatically carry over the habits of one environment into another. It is not uncommon among nonacademic teachers, though, even some with years of experience in the teaching of adults. The no-feedback fault can be overcome with the help of such behaviors as these:

Keep a watchful eye on your audience, and they'll let you know if you've lost them.

Develop a perceptive eye so that you can become aware of the uniqueness of the individuals in the class.

Never lecture for more than forty minutes. Break your lecture down into ten-minute segments and pause after each of these breaks to ask for questions and comments (see Chapter 4).

Instead of having a final exam at the end of the class, schedule short quizzes and other exercises throughout the class.

Where there is a term paper, have learners present an outline at least halfway through the course. This will reinforce teacher-learner communication and provide an opportunity to pick up on any weaknesses in the project while there is time to do something about them.

Always collect class and homework assignments and return them with grades (where required) and comments.

If the participants in the teaching-learning transaction are not learning, entertain the possibility that it is the fault of your teaching and set about making some changes.

Overcoming the kind of teaching faults catalogued in this chaper begins in the teacher's consciousness, with an attitudinal change. Ordinary consciousness, as psychologist Robert Ornstein notes, is "each individual's own private construction."[3] The teacher, in the act of teaching, draws upon this private construction; the learners, in the act of learning, bring their private constructions into the transaction. When these separate realities meet and stimulate each other, the learning that takes place is a vital and mutually enriching process.

REFERENCES

1. Clara M. Argyle and M. Cook, 1976, in Marianne La France and Clara Mayo, *Moving Bodies,* Wadsworth, Belmont, Calif., 1978.
2. Robert A. Segal, "What Is Good Teaching and Why Is There So Little of It?" *Chronicle of Higher Education,* September 24, 1979.
3. Robert E. Ornstein, *The Psychology of Consciousness,* Freeman, San Francisco, 1972, p. 17.

Chapter 8

TEACHING SPECIAL GROUPS

From its earliest beginnings, adult education has served two clienteles: the general audience and the special group. The men and women who came together to hear Ralph Waldo Emerson or William Jennings Bryan on the Chautauqua circuit were a general audience, as are those who gather today at seminars, workshops, and lecture series dealing with topics in the arts, sciences, or humanities that appeal to an educated, relatively affluent sector of the population. They are the people we think of as belonging to the American mainstream.

By contrast, the special group usually consists of those who for one reason or another are not part of the broad current of American life.* In the past, they were exemplified by the immigrants who studied English at night in the hope of lifting themselves out of their poverty by adapting to the American way of life. Today, spurred by concern with "rights" and "entitlements," special groups are proliferating and moving to the forefront of continuing education. They include women, ethnic minorities, the handicapped, urban youth, workers, the elderly, and the institutionalized. While there are overlaps among these groups and differences within, they have this in common: For the most part, they are seeking not primarily intellectual stimulus or personal fulfillment but the means of survival in an increasingly complex world. As in psychologist Abraham Maslow's five-level hierarchy of needs, they are struggling to meet their first- and second-level needs—survival and security—before going on to satisfy their social, achievement, and self-actualization needs.[1]

*An obvious exception are the professional groups, dealt with later in the chapter.

The major differences between these two groups of learners are demonstrated in the following table:

GENERAL AUDIENCE	SPECIAL GROUP
Diffuse	Contained
Fluctuating	Steady
Diverse interests	Focused interest
Ambivalent goals	Defined goals
Mainly voluntary	May be voluntary or involuntary
Usually fee-supported	Both fee- and subsidy-supported

ETHNIC MINORITIES: COPING WITH CULTURE SHOCK

As a teacher working with special groups, your "classroom" may be in a labor camp for Mexican migrant workers or a makeshift meeting room in a factory, a prison, a hospital, or a nursing home for the elderly. Particularly if your learners are members of ethnic minority groups, you may find yourself confronted with the challenge of making contact with people who are culturally different from yourself. Most teachers in continuing education identify with the mainstream culture: they are predominantly Caucasian, are educated, and have some achievement to their credit, in the form of academic degrees or professional attainment, which qualifies them for their teaching assignment. How does someone whose view of the world has been shaped by an upwardly mobile, middle-class society prepare to teach English as a Second Language or the essentials of American government to a group of Mexican farm laborers or automobile repair to urban blacks? One obvious answer is: Provide teachers who want to work with special groups with the appropriate training—a cross-cultural program, for example, as preparation for teaching ethnic minorities. Such programs are rare, however, and are usually designed by well-meaning educators who are also members of the majority culture and who share its perceptions and attitudes toward groups outside the mainstream.

As a consequence, in special-group education, the practice of patronizing the learners is a matter not only of style, but also of substance. A teacher describes her first experience with an intermediate ESL (English as a Second Language) class including Laotians, Iranians, Lebanese, and Chinese: "When I arrived in my classroom, I took a look at the reading material I had been provided with and was appalled to discover it was *The Three Bears!*" This is not an uncommon experience, sad to say; for some reason, people who lack a command of English are often regarded as also lacking adult intelligence and comprehension. Although, as suggested in the previous chapter, materials should not be so advanced as to discourage learners, neither should they be at a level intended for first or second graders. The experience of the teacher quoted above simply reinforces the importance of checking out all resources in advance and incorporating them in your planning.

Cultural condescension has also entered into the conflict over the teaching of Black English. It is not possible here nor would it be useful to go into the various arguments that have surfaced on both sides of this highly controversial issue. They range from a psycholinguist's insistence that standard English is not a "better form of language or a more acceptable form, but rather a different form, accepted by the majority of people as the norm."[2] to an English professor's contention that "it is only a sentimental populism that can pronounce Black English 'a language' just as rich and useful as standard Anglo-American or any other tongue."[3] For the purpose of the teacher working with ethnic minorities, it is worth noting that the emerging consensus, such as it is, appears to be tilting toward the view that blacks and other minorities should be taught standard English but that the teacher should be familiar with the dialect that is to be replaced and should have a wholesome rather than a scornful attitude toward that dialect.

The "Cultural Deprivation" Syndrome

Teachers with a genuine commitment to the education of ethnic minorities would probably deny that they harbor any biases or patronizing attitudes toward their learners, but cultural conditioning is so deep and pervasive, it is often difficult to shed the assumptions and perceptions that have been developed over a lifetime. There is no need, even if it were possible, for the teacher to adopt the culture of the people he or she is teaching. You do not have to become an American Indian in order to teach American Indians. It is, however, highly desirable for the teacher to develop a heightened sensitivity to the culture of the minorities being taught and to be aware of the attitudes and behaviors that are responsible for the communication gap that often develops between teachers of one culture and learners of another.

One of the causes for this gap has been described as the "cultural deprivation" response of the American educational system to minorities. According to a leading authority on minority group history and culture, Jack D. Forbes, who is himself of Powhatan Indian descent, the failure of American education in regard to racial and cultural minorities stems from the traditional approach that views the minority groups as "culturally deprived" and focuses the "blame" for failure upon the group. It is the minority group that must adjust, conform, and change;

the traditional program is considered sound and in need of no fundamental revision.[4]

Continuing education has, with the best intentions, adopted this approach in many of its compensatory programs, which are generally based upon the assumption that increased exposure to any learning environment together with an intensified remedial approach will solve or at least ameliorate the problem of "the disadvantaged" or "culturally deprived." The concept of cultural deprivation reflects a belief that black and Hispanic minority groups do not possess a culture that can be utilized or enhanced by education. The minority group is deprived because members are not inheritors of the middle-class tradition, and it is the job of the teacher to make up for this deficiency.

These and similar assumptions should be carefully and critically examined by teachers from the majority culture who wish to teach minorities. Not all members of all minorities are bent on "making it" into American middle-class life. The resurgence of ethnic pride and identity in recent years has revealed that the aspirations of minorities today differ from those of the turn-of-the-century immigrants who sought in education a means of becoming Americanized. Today blacks, American Indians, Orientals, and other ethnic groups are looking to education to help them become responsible, self-sustained citizens, but they are not necessarily eager to surrender their cultural identities in order to fit into a common mold.

In fact, one of the fallacies teachers should be wary of is the perception of ethnic groups as if they were homogenous entities whose learning needs and capacities may differ from one group to another but are essentially the same within a particular culture. Black leader Bayard Rustin has identified three groups within the black community, each with distinct needs requiring different educational techniques and environments: (1) the poor, the unemployed, and those trapped in low-paying, dead-end jobs; (2) those having working-class jobs, including union members; (3) those who have some experience with college. The first group requires remedial education and job training; the second group, who may be reached through employee training programs, is likely to be interested in such subjects as labor history, politics, and occupational health and safety; group three, which includes those who dropped out of college or were not able to go beyond the junior college level, is motivated mainly by the desire to complete their education and receive a college degree.[5]

Differences such as these exist among all minority cultures. The teacher who works with these groups should make these distinctions as early as possible. The needs assessment takes on added importance in special-group teaching as a means of providing cues for the teacher's approach to the learners. The following is a model of a needs assessment that is brief and simple and at the same time provides the basic information the teacher requires. It was developed for an ESL class attended by Mexican migrant workers at a labor camp in California:

Name:_____ Age: _____
What is your job here?
How many months/years have you lived at this camp?
Have you lived in other parts of the United States?
Where do you usually live?
What are some of the greatest differences between your life here and your life in
    Mexico?
What are some of the problems you find here?
Have you studied English before? If so, where and for how long?
Why do you want to learn English?

Approaches and Teaching Strategies

The cardinal rule for teaching people who are culturally different is: Learn as much as you can about their culture. This includes at least a minimal acquaintance with their native language, the history of their country of origin; their literature, religion, and values. The preferred training for instructors of minorities is in anthropology and sociology. Some of this information can also be obtained from the learners themselves, through discussions on these topics in class. People from ethnic minority backgrounds are usually pleased to talk about their cultures with someone who is genuinely interested; it gives them an opportunity to "teach the teacher," thus enhancing their role in the learning process.

Specific teaching approaches and strategies gathered from experienced teachers of minorities and researchers in the field include:

In planning an educational program for minorities, the teacher should consult members of that minority group.

Realize that people belonging to ethnic minorities are often in need of raising their self-esteem. They have a low tolerance for even minor defeats or setbacks, and a negative attitude may be a cover-up for a fear of failure. The teacher's attitude should be positive and encouraging.

Select materials that are relevant to the learners' lives. A teacher with a class of recently arrived Vietnamese chose as a reading exercise a poem entitled "Homesick" written by a child in the Warsaw ghetto. The teacher describes the exercise as follows: "First I read it so they could get a sense of its shape and sound; then they asked me questions about words and meaning; then we read it together like a chant, and finally, they read it individually. As a follow-up, I asked them to compose their own short poems on the same idea."

Supplementary materials utilized in class, as well as library resources, should include numerous minority-related items (magazines, newspapers, books, photographs, recordings, films) in order to provide cross-cultural experiences for learners and provide an atmosphere relevant to the learner's heritage.

Make maximum use of the cultural assets and skills of the learners. A class in music appreciation attended by blacks should include jazz composed by black musicians, or if the learners are Mexican-Americans, Mexican mariachi music.

Many brown-skinned and black-skinned persons suffer psychologically to some degree from the tendency to exalt light skin and blondeness in the United States. This feeling can be counteracted by the use of periodicals, films, books, and other materials of nonwhite origin, such as East Indian, Latin American, and Japanese items.

The contributions of ethnic minority cultures should be treated as integral and valuable parts of our common legacy and not as bits of exotica relevant solely to the minorities themselves.

As a result of their historic experience, many ethnic minority persons tend to be passive, particularly in a classroom presided over by someone whom they perceive as an authority figure—a teacher belonging to the majority culture. The most effective techniques are proactive, encouraging learners to participate in the learning activities and thus develop initiative.

The growing populations of ethnic minorities in many parts of the United States suggest that teaching opportunities in this field will be increasing during the 1980s. Teachers who are qualified to take on instructional assignments with minority groups should find this a promising and personally gratifying career.

WOMEN: LEARNERS IN TRANSITION

As a clientele for continuing education, women, although numerically in the majority, can be compared in certain respects to ethnic minorities: they have a history of being excluded from politics, business, industry, and the professions; they have a shaky self-concept as a result of being confined to narrow, stereotyped roles; they have been socially conditioned toward passivity; and they are looking to education primarily to help them gain a footing in the shifting sands of changing roles and a precarious economy.

Teaching women as a special group begins, as does all teaching of adults, with the commandment, Know thy audience. Who are these women who are flooding into continuing education, and what do they hope to gain? A seasoned designer of women's programs describes them this way:

We are dealing with an elusive group of people whose senses and sensibilities have been honed and sharpened in the last decade. We have women hostile to the women's movement—but they're still out there looking around—and taking courses. They are not Women's Libbers but they would like to be more assertive in dealing with the plumber and the manager of the supermarket. We have some who are supersensitive to being patronized in the classroom ... whose backs will straighten and eyes will flash every time you use the generic "he"or refer to them as "girls." Whether you like it or not, that's your audience.[6]

In other words, they are as diversified as any other group of adult learners, while sharing, as a special group, some common needs and goals. They include women with careers as well as housewives. Those over thirty-five, who make up the larger part of the continuing education audience, are reentering the work force in droves and are therefore taking courses to develop or increase their earning power.* A recent Roper poll found that the primary reason women work is for money; only 14 percent said they work for self-fulfillment. As more and more women find themselves divorced or widowed or needing to maintain the family's standard of living in an inflationary time, they echo the words of a divorced mother of three: "I don't feel any need to prove myself—just to eat."[7]

What kind of education are these "new women" looking for? Glance through the continuing education catalogs of two-year and four-year institutions and you will see courses like these: Career Strategies for Women in the Wholesale Apparel Industry, Career Planning for Women, New Career Options for Women, Financial Management for Women, The Managerial Woman, The Entrepreneurial Woman. Noticeably absent or diminished are programs that flourished in the sixties and early seventies on women's history and consciousness raising.

The changing emphasis in continuing education for women throughout the country can be illustrated by two examples. The first is the Continuing Education for Women Center at George Washington University, Washington, D.C.

The Center was launched in 1964 with the objective of helping women to establish or reevaluate their sense of direction and purpose and to assess objectively their interests and abilities. This original self-awareness program has expanded over the years to include one-year career certificate programs designed to help women gain skills in selected employment areas such as publishing, landscape architecture, management, and legal assistance.[8]

The second example is the highly innovative Womanschool established in New York City in 1975. Womanschool does not have degree-granting authority, and its short-term, noncredit courses are designed to meet the immediate practical needs of its students. At its inception, the curriculum consisted of such courses as Being and Becoming Single, Successful Couple Relationships, and Middlescence—The Years After Forty. Today there are more than forty courses nearly all of which emphasize career training, placement, and advancement. The

---

*In the last decade, more than 3 million women between the ages of twenty-five and fifty-four from all classes and ethnic groups have obtained jobs at various levels. During this period, the number of women who head households, according to data compiled by the Women's Bureau of the U.S. Department of Labor, increased by 57 percent. The result is that one-fourth of all American households are headed by women.

school's highly successful placement center works with corporations and institutions in the New York area to locate jobs for its students. The proportion of Womanschool students with full-time jobs was about 75 percent in 1978, and has been steadily increasing.[9]

The growing interest in marketable skills among women is a significant indicator for teachers who are interested in serving this group of learners. Men and women who have gained experience in careers or professional fields, particularly those that have not been traditionally regarded as women's occupations, and who can communicate their experience effectively will find the welcome mat out wherever women come together to continue their education.

In planning and conducting courses for women, the teacher should consider the following points:

> Women as learners are eager, responsive, and highly motivated; however, many are combining their studies with household and child care responsibilities that account for the citing of fatigue as their greatest learning problem. Class time should be used with maximum efficiency; assignments outside of class should be geared realistically to the pressures and time limitations of the learners' lives.
> Women reentering the world of education and work are often in need of counseling before they can make the necessary adaptations; the teacher should be alert to this need and refer learners to the appropriate counseling services.
> Whenever possible, occupational training should include field trips to the sites of the careers and vocations being studied. Women making the transition from the home to the world of work need to be familiarized with the actuality of the working environment—the look and feel of factories, offices, television studies, computer facilities, and so on.
> Select guest speakers who can serve as stereotype-counteracting role models for the learners: for example, in a course on management for women, the teacher invited a top woman executive and her male secretary to address the class on new relationships in the executive suite.
> Examine all learning materials in advance to be sure they are free of sexist attitudes.
> See Appendix E for resources available for women's programs.

As in the case of ethnic minorities, women need a supportive learning environment. They need help in making what is often a difficult and painful transition from an earlier conditioning that prepared them to live as dependents and at the service of others to the realities of a society in which there are smaller families, a high divorce rate, longer lives, and an inflationary economy that is making two-income families the norm. Elizabeth Hardwick has observed:

> Society does not want women to lead a long life in the home. It is not prepared to support them and cannot give the old style true sanction. Children do not want their parents' lives to be given to them forever. Husbands cannot take the responsibilities for wives as an immutable duty, ordained by nature. Women's liberation suits society

much more than society is prepared to admit. The wife economy is as obsolete as the slave economy.[10]

In this transition from an obsolete society to the world that is emerging in the 1980s, teachers in the expanding field of women's education have a pivotal role to play.

THE ELDERLY AS LEARNERS

Many old people prefer to be hypochondriacs, niggards, pedants, applauders of the past or else eternal adolescents—all lamentable substitutes for the illumination of the self, but inevitable consequences of the delusion that the second half of life must be governed by the principles of the first.

Carl Jung*

What about those old people who do not wish to belong to any of the categories that Jung set forth in the above statement? What learning opportunities are there for older adults who want to continue being active, involved, and in touch with the present and the future? What problems do they face as participants in the learning process?

The very fact that the elderly have been set aside as a special group for the purposes of learning testifies to the widespread influence of ageism in American society. A 1975 study sponsored by the National Council on Aging reported that only 29 percent of the public aged eighteen to sixty-four viewed older persons as "very bright and alert" and only 35 percent viewed them as "very good at getting things done."[11] Older adults suffer from the handicap of being defined as the less productive members of a society that values those who contribute to the Gross National Product. For many, retirement becomes "aimless wandering—the consequence of the national misconception that life's ultimate door prize is security and that leisure is an unskilled occupation."[12]

Work Policy

There are hopeful signs that these negative attitudes are changing thanks to the demographic phenomenon that has come to be known as "the graying of America." Older adults are increasing both in numbers and as a proportion of the total population. In 1900, only 3.1 million persons were sixty-five and over, representing 4.1 percent of the population. By 1975, 22.4 million adults were sixty-five or over, representing 10.5 percent of the population. If the present low birthrate

*Carl G. Jung, *Psychological Reflections,* Princeton University Press, Princeton, N.J., 1970.

continues, by the year 2000 about 31 million Americans will be sixty-five and over, representing 11.7 percent of the total population.[13]

This demographic change is affecting American postsecondary education in several ways: Courses in gerontology are springing up around the country; since the 1970s, the number of postsecondary institutions offering such courses has multiplied 25 times. Programs specifically designed for older adults, such as Elderhostel, are increasing. The prospect of a growing postretirement population has brought about a reassessment in continuing education of the kind of courses being offered as well as of scheduling and financing.

Myths and Misconceptions

As with other special groups, there is the tendency to homogenize the elderly, to lump them together, as if the adding on of years leveled out individual differences. In fact, as recent research in gerontology tells us, not only do people become more individuated as they grow older, but the aging process itself is far from uniform. Biological, psychological, socioeconomic, and environmental factors all enter into the differences in the way people age. Also, cross-cultural studies on aging are producing data that suggest that while certain manifestations of aging are inevitable others are primarily cultural.

A widespread misconception about aging that is of particular concern to teachers of adults is the belief that intelligence deteriorates in the later years. "Senility" is the scare word that rouses anxieties and self-doubt in older people who would like to continue their education but are uncertain about their learning capability. What light does recent research shed on the relationship between aging and intelligence?

A leader in the field of gerontology, Lissy Jarvik, professor of psychiatry at UCLA, has found, in her studies of an aging population over a period of several years, that there is no decline in knowledge or reasoning ability—not only into the thirties and forties but into the sixties and seventies as well. The studies showed that, while there was a slowing down in speed of reaction, there was no decline in mental ability; also, that loss of memory, the most common complaint among the elderly, is often due to inadequate learning in the first place, or it may be due to faulty vision or hearing, inattention, or trying to learn at too fast a speed. Mental deterioration among the elderly, according to Dr. Jarvik, is often a misdiagnosis for loneliness and depression, conditions that frequently can be helped by counseling and psychotherapy.[14]

Here is how a professor of biology who teaches in the Elderhostel project, a summer program of educational hosteling for people over sixty, describes his experience in teaching older adults: "When hosteling began, I did the first year with some trepidation. I didn't know what I was dealing with or whether I would be able to reach old people. I've found them an absolute delight to teach. Their enthusiasm is very high. They have a good time and obviously like to learn.[15]

Learning Needs of the Elderly

What do older adults want to learn, and how do they want to go about learning? Although there is as much—or more—diversity among the elderly as in any other group, there are also some common threads in their learning preferences:

> There is a need for continuity as the "inescapable experiential product of a kind of process which ties the events and ideas of one period to those of the next.[16] A thematic, interdisciplinary approach is more likely to succeed than the breaking down of subject matter into separate compartments.
> The program should tap some deep interest or need.
> It should bolster confidence in the participants' ability to learn.
> It should be noncompetitive.
> There should be plenty of opportunity for social interaction.
> Counseling should be provided as necessary to help learners relate instruction to personal needs.
> Learners should be encouraged to proceed at their own pace.
> Whenever possible, programs should be scheduled in the daytime in locations accessible to public transportation.
> Physical problems of the elderly should be taken into consideration: short breaks should be scheduled at reasonable intervals; reading and workbook materials should be selected which are available in large, easy-to-read print; particular attention should be given to comfortable ventilation and good lighting.

In time, colleges and universities may become community learning centers attended by people of all ages, and older adults who wish to continue learning will no longer have to do so as a special group. Meanwhile, the challenge to teachers working with the elderly is to stimulate and encourage what older people can accomplish as learners, with the ultimate aim of integrating them into the mainstream so that they can live productive lives and provide healthy models of aging for the young.

TEACHING PROFESSIONALS

Professionals stand apart from the other special groups discussed in this chapter in several significant respects: They have not been denied educational opportunities; on the contrary, they have been able to pursue their education to the highest level, as required by the profession of their choice. Regardless of their ethnic or socioeconomic origins, their professional status places them squarely in the main-stream and, in such professions as medicine and law, in the middle- to upper-middle-income brackets. Continuing their education is a matter of professional rather than personal survival.

Also, the expansion of continuing education for professionals in recent years is due not only to the needs of the learners, but even more so, to the growth of mandatory certification and relicensure regulations. These regulations represent a response by state legislatures to public concern over competency in doctors, lawyers, and other professionals. The explosion of new knowledge and technolo-gies in the professions, particularly the health sciences, has intensified the demand for evidence that the professional is keeping up with developments in the field. State legislatures are now requiring continuing education for at least half the licensed professions, and occupations that have never before required licensing are being included, often at their own insistence, in mandatory regulations certify-ing competency. As a result, continuing education for professionals, which was a relatively minor part of the college and university extension curriculum, is beginning to dominate these programs. At the same time, colleges and universities are losing what was once a virtual monopoly of professional education to a host of competitors, among them professional associations, private firms, and even community colleges for occupations such as nursing or the training of paraprofes-sionals, especially in law and the health sciences.

Mandated Education: Pros and Cons

The growth of mandatory education has made this a major and controversial issue in the education of professionals. Those who are in favor of the mandatory approach, or who consider it more or less inevitable, maintain that it serves the public interest, since without such formal control, many professionals would not pursue continuing education on their own. Considering how rapidly knowledge, skills, and technologies become obsolescent in most professions today, it is essen-tial for society, so the argument goes, that professionals be required to keep up to date with new developments in their fields.

Opponents of mandated study maintain that this type of force feeding can have reverse effects. By being forced to attend courses which they may feel do not serve their particular needs, practitioners may develop a negative attitude toward the idea of continuing their education. Those who argue against mandatory study suggest in its place a program of self-study, which would rely on the professional's self-motivation, professional pride, and desire to serve society.

Another suggested alternative to mandatory education is competency determi-nation. Proponents of this approach favor periodic evaluation of professionals through examination, performance evaluation, and/or other agreed-upon methods of assessment.

Since, from all present indications, mandatory education is the approach that will prevail, teachers in professional continuing education will find themselves increasingly serving a captive audience. This situation places an especially heavy premium on flexibility. The teacher must be prepared to deal with individuals whose motivation levels range from high to low to nonexistent, as illustrated in Cyril Houle's classification (Figure 8.1). With learners as diverse as these, it is easy to see why teaching professionals is a special kind of challenge, requiring a high standard of preparation and a strong personal commitment.

FIGURE 8.1   A Classification of the Members of a Profession.

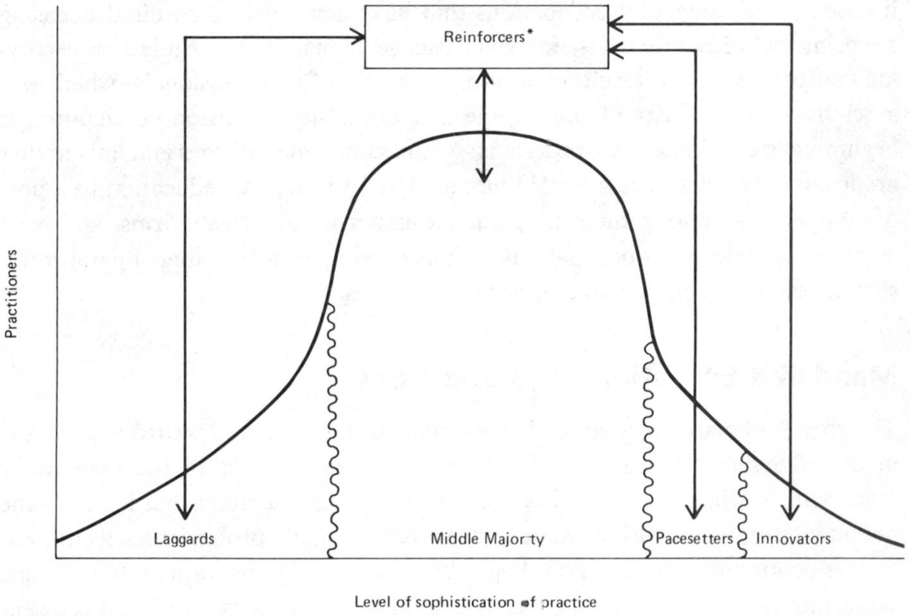

Practitioners

Reinforcers*

Laggards   Middle Majority   Pacesetters   Innovators

Level of sophistication of practice

From the address "The Nation of Continuing Professional Education" by Cyril O. Houle, professor of education, The University of Chicago, at the APhA Seminar for Continuing Education Personnel.

New Teaching Opportunities

Teachers of professionals in continuing education have usually been recruited from research faculty of institutions of learning or from the profession itself. In the past few years, however, there have been developments in the professions which appear to be opening up new teaching opportunities for nonprofessionals. Chief among these is the mounting criticism, much of it by professionals themselves, directed against the isolation and overspecialization of the professions.

There are complaints that lawyers are trained as narrow technicians, which is seen as one of the causes of the widening gap between law and justice. A doctor and professor of medicine charges:

> Overspecialization is a continuing problem in American medical schools, but an equally serious flaw is their tendency to produce too many doctors who lack the human—and in medicine's case professionally essential—virtue of empathy, understanding and compassion. For various reasons, many of today's doctors simply fail to recognize basic human needs and therefore neglect to treat the whole patient.[17]

Reacting to this type of criticism, continuing education has begun offering such programs as The Engineer in Society, Ethical Issues in the Law, The Physician and the Urban Community. These programs, which concern themselves with values and social issues, are designed to broaden and, in effect, humanize the professions. As such courses proliferate, and it appears likely that they will, teachers of adults whose training is in the social sciences and the humanities will be able to bring their talents and energies to a special learning area that, like other special teaching, offers an as yet barely explored potential for a creative teaching-learning experience.

REFERENCES

1. Abraham Maslow, *Toward a Psychology of Being,* Van Nostrand, Princeton, N.J. 1968.
2. Benice Lindo, *Black Ghetto Dialect,* Instant Phonics, Los Angeles, 1972.
3. Richard Mitchell, *Less Than Words Can Say,* Little, Brown, Boston, 1979.
4. Jack D. Forbes, *Education of the Culturally Different: A Multicultural Approach,* Far West Laboratory for Educational Research and Development, Berkeley, Calif., 1969.
5. Bayard Rustin, "Continuing Education: Beyond the Walls of Higher Education," National University Extension Association Conference, Tucson, Ariz., March 20, 1977.
6. Sallie O'Neill, *Continuing Education for Women,* Proceedings of the Continuing Education Goes to Market Conference, UCLA Extension, Los Angeles, 1976.
7. Emily Greenspan, "Work Begins at 35," *New York Times Magazine,* July 6, 1980.
8. Clare Grosgebauer, "The Little Courses That Grew," *American Education,* June 1977, pp. 10–13.
9. Nan Robertson, "School for Women Takes a Different Course," *New York Times,* May 6, 1978.
10. Elizabeth Hardwick, "Domestic Manners," *Daedalus,* Winter 1978, p. 10.
11. Study by Harris and Associates, 1975, National Council on Aging, Washington, D.C.
12. Willard W. Wirtz, *The Boundless Resource: A Prospectus for an Education-Work Policy,* New Republic Book Co., Washington, D.C., 1975.
13. *Lifelong Learning and Public Policy,* a report prepared by the Lifelong Learning Project, U.S. Dept. of Health, Education and Welfare, Washington, D.C., 1978.

14. Lissy F. Jarvik, Carl Eisdorfer and June Blum, eds. *Intellectual Functioning in Adults: Psychological and Biological Influences,* Springer Publishing, New York, 1973.
15. Henry T. Yost, quoted in Zoe Ingalis, "We're Not Dead Yet," *The Chronicle of Higher Education,* July 21, 1980.
16. Barbara G. Myerhoff and Andrei Simic, *Life's Career—Aging: Cultural Variations on Growing Old,* Sage Publications, Beverly Hills, Calif., 1978.
17. Forrest H. Adams, "He'll Make A Good Doctor—If He Gets In," *Los Angeles Times,* April 31, 1978.

Chapter 9

ETHICAL ISSUES IN ADULT EDUCATION

The teacher of adults is often confronted at a personal level with ethical and moral dilemmas that are a reflection of unresolved problems in continuing education. The idea that teachers should be insulated from social pressures—which is the rationale for tenure in higher education—simply does not work out as a day-to-day reality in the teaching of nontraditional adult students. The teacher cannot escape the fallout from the policies and practices that are carried out by the educational institution or other organization under whose aegis he or she is teaching. If it is an extension division of a college or university, the teacher may also be affected by the campus administration's stance in regard to such matters as credit, grading, and degrees.

The growth of continuing education in recent years plus the heightened competition for this increasingly attractive market have had both positive and negative effects: on the credit side, there are the innovative programs designed to attract nontraditional students; on the debit side, there are questionable practices and a huckstering approach, especially in recruiting students. A Veterans Administration report submitted to Congress in 1979 stated: "Some [schools] seem to have become less stuffy, more responsive, practical, adaptable and lively; others (sometimes the same institutions) more mercenary and lacking any fixed standard but survival."[1]

Financial pressures are primarily responsible for fostering an environment in which ethical and moral dilemmas abound. When education is regarded as a "business," and educators talk in terms of "market conditions" and refer to students as "consumers," conscientious teachers may find themselves in a bind as they attempt to reconcile commercialism with the teaching-learning activity. Mark Harris, novelist and English teacher, describes his experience at a high-fee creative writing conference where he was told by the dean to assign topics to the students. Harris protested that he couldn't teach writing that way, that writers, however young or inexperienced, must tap their own resources. The dean insisted that Harris go ahead with the procedure of assigned topics because "that was the way it was advertised" and "the name of the game is consumerism."[2]

A Numbers Game

Adult education, which operates largely as a pay-as-you-go proposition, must have extrasensitive antennae in order to pick up the signals indicating what sort of educational fare "they," the people in the community being served, are willing to pay for. Numbers of enrollments are crucial to subsidized as well as fee-supported education, since government support is based on attendance. What this means, simply, is that, wherever or whatever you may be teaching, unless a specified minimum number of students are enrolled, you will not have a class to teach. This seems obvious enough, particularly from the point of view of those administering the programs, but it often comes as a shock to a new teacher, looking forward to that first teaching experience and having spent several weeks or months in careful preparation, to discover that the class has been cancelled for lack of enrollments.

Truth in Advertising

Teachers and administrators may have their differences at times, but one thing they are in complete agreement about is the need to do everything possible to boost enrollments, at least to the required minimum. What does "everything possible" encompass? To begin with, there should be a vigorous advertising and promotion campaign. Here the agreement between the administrator and the teacher may falter somewhat, since the administrator has a large number of courses to promote whereas the teacher is convinced that his or her course is the most important and exciting entry in the curriculum and deserves star billing.

In whatever way this difference is negotiated, there is at times an irresistible temptation to hype up the advertising and publicity for the course, to make it as alluring and irresistible as possible. In recent years, continuing education catalog copy has begun to resemble Madison Avenue's more glittering efforts. Courses, seminars, and workshops are described in terms usually reserved for cosmetics and breakfast cereals. Career and vocational programs strongly hint, if they do not come right out with it, that a job or career awaits the participant at the conclusion of the program. An advertisement for a national "nontraditional college marketing seminar" addresses academic administrators as follows: "The question is: how do you attract more students? One answer: use the same techniques and ideas successfully used to sell other concepts."

A recurring complaint among adult students is "course not as advertised." The catalog copy for a lecture series says that there will be several guest speakers, each an outstanding authority in the field, whereas actually only one or two guest speakers appear, neither one of whom can be fairly described as outstanding or authoritative. Or in the copy for a specialty writing course, students are assured that there is a promising market for articles in this subject area, whereas in fact the opportunities for selling such articles are few and far between.

In the euphoria of planning a course and with the understandable desire to attract substantial enrollments, exaggerations and even out-and-out misstatements may find their way into the advertising and publicity. Even at the risk of losing a few enrollments or having a class cancelled, teachers should see it to that their courses are advertised with the strictest accuracy. Nothing should be promised that cannot be delivered. Each word should be carefully weighed to make sure that no false expectations are being raised. In many cases, teachers are involved in the advertising and promotion of their courses from the beginning, but where this is not so, they should make every effort to check out the catalog copy and other promotional materials in advance and eliminate any hype or misleading statements. At stake is nothing less than the integrity of the teacher as well as that of the organization offering the course.

Body Counts

Let's assume that you are teaching a course in conversational French. The course has been designed for those who have some facility with the language, and it has been described accordingly in the catalog. You have been advised that it will take a minimum of fifteen students to carry the class. There are sixteen students at the opening session, but as it turns out, three of them are not at the requisite level of conversational facility. They would like to stay in the class anyway, since they feel they will be motivated to move more quickly toward the level of the others in the class. What do you do?

Problems like these turn up from time to time, presenting the teacher with an either-or situation: either decide in favor of keeping the students in the class, thus maintaining the class, recognizing, however, that they will probably slow down the pace of classwork and act as a drag on the others; or turn away the three students, thus losing the class and disappointing the other thirteen. Those teachers who decide in favor of keeping the unqualified students in the class can rationalize the decision on the basis of meeting their obligation to the larger number of qualified students who wish to take the course. In attempting to intermix two groups of students of widely differing abilities, however, where the value of the learning experience depends upon a fairly equal level of capability among the participants, the teacher invites the risk of shortchanging both groups.

In the type of example given above, the problem might be resolved in any of the following ways without diluting or weakening the class: The administrator supervising the course might decide to stretch the budget and maintain the class below the prescribed minimum. Or, as sometimes happens, the teacher might agree to accept a reduced compensation. Occasionally, when a class is threatened by cancellation, each student contributes an additional sum above the fee to meet the budgetary requirements for the class. The issue is essentially one of fair dealing, and the conscientious teacher will always seek some modus operandi in which survival is not purchased at the cost of lowering learning standards.

Conflict of Interest

Ideally, teaching should involve the whole person, and all external pulls or pressures that might distort the process should be excluded. Full-time teachers, for whom teaching is a lifetime career, are in a position to invest themselves wholly in their work. This is not usually the case with part-time teachers who have other occupations on which they depend for their livelihood.

In profiling part-time teachers (see Chapter 1), we have observed that these instructors bring to students the benefits of practical experience. This is particularly valuable in career and vocational or other skill-related areas or in the teaching of leisure-time pursuits, such as sports, crafts, or gourmet cooking. On the other side of the coin, where teaching is, in essence, a "moonlighting" activity, there is always the possibility that it will be subordinated to the demands of the teacher's principal occupation.

A few examples drawn from actual experience suggest the kind of ethical dilemmas that part-time teachers may find themselves confronted by:

An ambitious young politician is teaching a course on current issues in local government. The course is being given for credit, the grade to be based mainly upon a term paper due at the final session. One student in the class is a member of the local school board and has community connections that are of crucial importance to the instructor's political career The school board member turns in a paper that falls far below the criteria for a passing grade. What does the instructor do?

A reporter for the community's major newspaper is teaching a course on legal and ethical issues in journalism. The family that owns the newspaper has vast agricultural holdings, and the editorial columns have been denouncing an attempt on the part of the legislature to ban a pesticide suspected of causing cancer. When a member of the class introduces this issue for discussion, how does the instructor handle it?

An attorney is teaching a course on environmental law. His major client is a large chemical manufacturing company that was recently tried and fined for contaminating the local water supply with toxic wastes. A member of the class chooses this case as the subject for his term paper, which he plans to publish in a legal journal. As part of his research, he wishes to conduct an in-depth interview with the instructor, who represented the company in the lawsuit. How open and honest is the instructor in providing information to the student?

A realtor is teaching a class in valuations procedures. Her office represents the owner of several large properties in the area which she, the instructor, knows to be highly overvalued. The members of the class have indicated that they are taking the course because they are interested in investing in real estate. In conducting an analysis of available properties in the area, how does the realtor deal with the evaluation of the properties represented by her office?

In cases like these, teachers are caught in a classic conflict-of-interest situation. If they are not willing to take a risk that might jeopardize their principal job or profession—and it is probably beyond the call of duty to expect them to do so —they should level with the class about the sensitivity of their position and how it affects their conduct in the specific case. Since most adult students are also working at jobs or professions, they can readily understand the kinds of ethical conflicts that are sometimes built into economic survival. In the first instance, the teacher gave the school board member a grade of "incomplete," suggesting that she rework the paper and resubmit it, offering suggestions for bringing it up to passing quality. She did so, and the instructor was able, with a clear conscience, to give the revised paper a passing grade.

The Hidden Agenda

Teachers of adults are not always motivated, as we observed in Chapter 1, by the pure love of teaching. Particularly in vocational and professional education, but also in other areas, it is not at all uncommon for the teacher to have a "hidden agenda" in which self-interest figures prominently. Among the examples offered earlier: the psychologist wishing to build up his practice; the author promoting her book, the realtor hoping to pick up a couple of new customers. One could add: the corporate executive hoping to enhance his company's image, the attorney looking for clients, the public official seeking votes in the upcoming election, and on and on.

All these people may have important information to communicate as well as first-rate teaching skills. Their self-interest may, and frequently does, coincide with the needs and objectives of their students, just as Adam Smith's famous "invisible hand" was supposed to bring private and public interests together, but the situation is undeniably fraught with a potential for abuse. Like conflict of interest, self-interest can erode the teaching process; it introduces a jarring element of exploitation into the interaction between teacher and learner which threatens the integrity of that relationship.

Instructors who are motivated by self-interest can still be effective and responsible as long as they face up honestly to why they are teaching and then make a rigorous effort to separate their self-serving motives from the teaching-learning transaction. This means that the psychologist does not interject at regular intervals a statement about the number of people he has helped in his private practice; the author does not urge her book upon the students nor does she place it on the reading list as a requirement if, in fact, it is not essential to the course; the corporate executive, in choosing actual companies for case studies, gives equal time to others than his own and presents a balanced view in every case; the public official does not discuss his own record in glowing terms while losing no opportunity to disparage that of his opponent.

Adult learners are quick to detect self-serving behavior on the part of an instructor. "He was always selling instead of telling" is the way one irritated responder summed it up on an evaluation of a class in retailing. By behaving so that the bond of trust between teacher and learners is maintained at all times, the teacher has an even better chance that the "invisible hand" will work to the benefit of his or her personal interest. From a position of mutual trust, learners may indeed seek out the psychologist's or attorney's or realtor's services when these are needed, may buy the author's book, may vote for the public official. These, however, must be regarded strictly as fringe benefits that may or may not result from a commitment to the learners' rather than the teachers' interests.

THE TEACHER AS A CHANGE AGENT

The teacher of adults shares with teachers at all levels of education a capacity for exercising influence. Regardless of the subject or the discipline, the act of teaching is directed toward enhancing the ability of learners to make choices. Says A. Bartlett Giamatti:

> That is the ethical impulse in teaching, to tell how to go about acquiring the material and then building the edifice of a belief. And from the architectonics of choices, a person will emerge, a person who knows how to cope with the radical loneliness we all inherit and the vast population of decisions we all live in, a person who can carry on.[3]

In helping that emerging person to build "the edifice of a belief," the teacher serves as an agent of change. This responsibility cannot be taken lightly; it affords the teacher an opportunity to have an impact upon problems and issues of the time and to delineate change so that we can have a better understanding of the past and of the world we are living in at present. Because of the dimensions and rapidity of change today, the teacher's capacity for influence has been greatly enlarged.

The role of the teacher, as Giamatti points out, is linked to "the nature of the institution in which the teaching is performed and to the nature of the society that the institution serves."[4] Pressures from the institution and the larger community may at times place the teacher in an ethically difficult position. In a number of instances teachers have refused to sign loyalty oaths in states where these were required. Religious, political, and other groups have tried to have courses eliminated from curriculums, books removed from reading lists, and teachers fired for offering instruction that was not in accord with the doctrines of the protesting group. In most cases of this type, teachers have found that, by resisting such pressures, they succeed in gaining the respect and support of colleagues and students and are able to continue teaching as their consciences dictate.

A problem of wider scope in the teaching of adults is finding a middle ground between controlling the mind of another person and letting that mind continue to be mired in ignorance and confusion. The teacher may wish to avoid paternalism or any suggestion of being an authority figure; but if the learners are permitted simply to go their own way, this is clearly an abdication of the teacher's responsibility to them. There are no conclusive or comprehensive solutions to problems like these. As in other areas of human activity, ethical problems in the teaching of adults must be dealt with according to the best judgment that the teacher can bring to each individual problem, along with the recognition that a degree of uncertainty and ambivalence is part of the price of being human.

REFERENCES

1. Jim Schutze and Bob Rivard, "Integrity Crisis Looms for Universities," *Dallas Times Herald,* reprinted in the *Los Angeles Times,* June 20, 1980.
2. Mark Harris, "What Creative Writing Creates Is Students," *New York Times Book Review,* July 27, 1980.
3. A. Bartlett Giamatti, "The American Teacher," *Harper's,* July 1980, p. 25.
4. Giamatti, op. cit., p. 28.

Chapter 10

A VIEW FROM TOMORROW

What will continuing education look like in the decade of the eighties and beyond? How will emerging technologies, changing patterns of work and leisure, new values and relationships determine the shape of teaching and learning in the future? As we approach the twenty-first century, we can begin to discern the outlines of a new learning environment that is taking form in the crucible of the present.

Assessing the future of education in America, we can predict with some certainty that adult education will continue to grow. Several social indicators point to this—particularly, the aging of the population and the ongoing need for retraining to keep up with new knowledge and advanced technologies. The time may not be far off when the notion of education being limited to a fixed number of years during one's youth will be discarded. Lifelong learning will become the norm, and education, as opposed to formal schooling, will serve as a source of continuous renewal and adaptation throughout our lives.

These trends are most likely to shape and direct the growth of adult education in the years ahead:

An increasing number of women will enter the work force. Unlike many women of today, who need preparation for entering or reentering the world of jobs and professions, tomorrow's women, the indications are, will be more concerned with the issue of whether their working life is in tune with their personal and family goals.[1]

Women can be expected to respond to the growing emphasis on the family without giving up their role as workers or their crusade for equal rights. The emerging family will take on a new value, says psychologist Eugene Kennedy, as "that unique structure in which occur essential and irreplaceable experiences that

102

shape a sense of human identity and significance."[2] It will not be the traditional family—homemaking mother, breadwinning father, and children. The growth of the single-parent family is a major demographic trend, and women learners of the future will include a substantial proportion of female heads of families with children. These women will need counseling services to help them prepare for new work-sex roles, as well as a curriculum that reflects their multidimensional lives.

Continued immigration, particularly to major cities, will underline the need for programs and for teachers of those programs to help the immigrants achieve the freer, more satisfying life that they came here in search of. At present, immigration accounts for one-fourth of net population growth in the United States. For immigrants, the most pressing need is to attain proficiency in English. This need will become more acute as Americans move toward an information society. As of now, approximately 55 percent of the work force is in the information business, which raises questions about the value of bilingual education: Does bilingual teaching deny students the chance for an economically useful education? The evidence suggests that those of foreign origin who do not gain a mastery of English may be precluded from getting a foothold on the first step of the economic ladder.[3]

Energy will continue to be costly as alternative sources are sought and developed. The energy crisis will affect the education of adults in two major respects: (1) There will be less travel for pleasure; instead, people will spend their leisure time taking a variety of courses at their local college and university continuing education divisions. Some of these courses will be in hard-core subject areas in the sciences and humanities and will require serious study toward a certificate or degree. Others, a larger proportion, will be directed toward personal development and a more creative use of leisure time. (2) The open-learning movement will continue to expand to serve those living at a distance from a college or university. People will take advantage of learning opportunities close to or within the walls of their homes: independent study; and courses by radio, television, newspaper, and even telephone, as in the Educational Telephone Network (ETN) at the University of Wisconsin, Madison. There will be a need for instructors who can design as well as teach courses for delivery to the "long-distance learner."

The fundamental nature of work will undergo drastic change. According to a report by the Organization for Economic Cooperation and Development (OECD) employers around the world are recognizing the need for employees to have more than mere technical training. When employees are given an opportunity to develop their whole personalities and engage in creative expression, the report says, they will contribute more to the economy. "Progress toward industrial democracy depends upon the existence of well-informed employees."[4] There will also be an increasing need for technical training, as computerization and other new technologies are introduced into the workplace. Employees will be given the chance to devote some of their working hours or extended sabbatical leaves to concentrated study. The OECD report predicts that employers will provide facilities where employees can study during the working day without loss of income. For the unemployed, government will sponsor training programs leading directly to jobs. In professional and paraprofessional fields, there is likely to be a growing demand for continuing education that will update knowledge and skills. To satisfy these demands, part-time teachers will be recruited from industry and the professions, and they will rely increasingly upon the new technologies in carrying out their teaching responsibilities.

The New Technologies and the Teaching of Adults

Visualize an adult learner several years from now. We'll call her Carol, and we'll say that she is a thirty-five-year-old woman with one child in third grade and two preschoolers. She left college in her sophomore year and now wishes to obtain a degree in liberal arts, after which she plans to enter law school. Her two younger children attend preschool in the mornings, her best time for studying.

Watch her now as she settles down in her living room to concentrate on a course in American history. She sits in a plastic carrel with a screen in front of her and consoles on three sides. A Viewdata on cable channel C slowly unfolds on the screen, listing the morning's programs. Her history program is on channel E. The professor, who is on the faculty of a university several hundred miles away, begins the lecture. As he proceeds, he asks questions of and invites comments from the learners, who are scattered over a wide geographical area.

Carol has a two-way adaptor on her TV set which enables her to respond to what is being presented on the screen. Responding is done by means of a keypad that, in addition to having thirty channel-selector buttons, has five response buttons by which learners can "touch in" their responses to the instructor's questions. Carol responds to several of the history professor's questions and also asks a question to which he provides an answer.

When the history lesson is over, Carol takes from a shelf an object that looks like a thick, silvery phonograph record—a videodisk—and clamps it into a playback machine that scans it with a laser. Turning her chair around to the other side of the carrel, she switches on a microcomputer with a pale green screen. She presses a command key on the keyboard, and on the computer screen the following sentence appears: "Which frame would you like to review?"

She indicates her choice by pressing a number on the keyboard; turning back to the disk player, she watches as a set of multiple-choice questions appear on the screen. She responds to the questions on the keyboard, and the computer punches out a card with her score.[5]

This may seem like an Orwellian fantasy, but some educators, especially those with experience in open learning, are prophesying that new communications technologies will revolutionize American education and that the time for this revolution is not far off. Says Robert McCabe of Miami-Dade Community College:

> I believe that individualization of instruction, through a combination of two-chip computers and videodiscs, with home TV receivers already in place, may be the wave of the future. The student population of the eighties will be much more varied—in age and in every other way—than today's student body. They will require not the mass delivery of courses, but new kinds of interactive, individualized programming.[6]

Emerging technologies that have been identified as promising areas for adult education include:

Teleconferencing
Computer-assisted instruction
Computer-managed instruction
Discs
Cable, including two-way
One-and one-half-inch formats for broadcast and on-site use, respectively
Satellites
Home video systems
Minicam
Radio (reemerging)
Audio tapes
Audio cassettes and slides[7]

The place these technologies may occupy in the future can be estimated by glancing at a sampling of some current open-learning activities: The Extension Division of the University of California at San Diego has linked its campus resources to those of book publishers, film and television producers, and public television channels to develop telecourses that are presented for credit in cooperation with other educational institutions.

The University of Mid-America, founded as a regional consortium in 1974, produces telecourses covering a wide range of subjects from accounting and consumerism to the history of Japan and the American Revolution. Course development teams include scholars, instructional designers, researchers, writers, producers, and evaluators. UMA's regional base is in the process of being expanded into a National Open University.

The University of Missouri Extension utilizes 19-inch color television monitors and videocassette playback units to deliver a variety of programs to the 20 geographical extension areas in the state's 114 counties.

IBM, which invests heavily in employee training, has established a network of computer-assisted instruction for its maintenance engineers around the world. The engineers are given access to terminals that provide them with updated information on new technologies.

At Stanford University, an IBM 1620 computer has been used to teach singing. The computer prints out a series of notes which the student sings to the beat of a metronome. The computer is programmed to compare the student's pitch with the true pitch so that the student can decide whether to repeat the exercise or go on to new material.

The British Open University, the model for many open-learning systems in America and other countries, offers individualized instruction to a mass public through a comprehensive educational technology that combines books, written assignments, computer grading, counseling, and summer seminars with supplementary programs or "sunrise semesters" presented every day on the radio and television networks of the British Broadcasting Corporation. Enrollments are approximately 65,000. To date, more than 15,000 people have earned B.A. degrees through the system.

Even from these few examples, one can perceive the potential benefits as well as the dangers of utilizing these communication technologies in education. Proponents of new technologies point to the advantage of bringing to millions of people the talents of outstanding educators. Educational levels, they claim, will be raised throughout society. Remote communities and rural areas will have access to instruction of the highest quality. Learning will become truly a lifelong pursuit, an integral part of the individual's daily life, available at home or in the workplace.

One educator foresees a university that

> might conceivably make available its special strengths in fields for which the intellectual and other resources best equip it and defer to its sister institutions in fields for which they are better suited, without feeling the need for comprehensive coverage that today often leads to intellectual inflation, depreciated values and a waste that universities can ill afford.[8]

The prospects for the teacher are also painted in glowing colors by the protechnologists. They depict the teachers of tomorrow as skilled educational technologists creating videotapes or writing computer-assisted instructional programs for millions of students. These teachers will be sought after by the corporations that distribute or broadcast such programs, and their status and financial rewards will be greatly augmented. It has even been suggested that, in a telecommunications society, successful teachers probably will earn as much as film stars do today.[9]

The Problem of Passivity

Whether or not these euphoric projections will one day become a reality, we can already begin to perceive some of the ways in which teaching and learning are likely to be affected by the so-called telecommunications revolution. Educators who are less than enthusiastic about learning-through-television foresee an increase in passivity among learners, a loss of the benefits that flow from personal interaction between learners and teacher and among learners themselves.

The problem of learner passivity is of the greatest concern to adult educators who have their eye on the future. A technological approach is the two-way adaptor or interactive mechanism that Carol, our hypothetical learner of tomorrow, was using and that has been experimented with in a few places, among them Columbus, Ohio, and Reading, Pennsylvania. It is still too early to draw any conclusions from these experiments in regard to the new equipment's effect on learner passivity. It is becoming apparent, however, that as with other educational systems, there are certain trade-offs for teachers and learners.

The teacher conducting a telecourse often works with prepackaged materials. Open-university course materials include study guides that provide a set of clearly defined goals and competencies designed to measure achievement and award credit. These materials incorporate the kinds of decisions that normally preoccupy the teacher: how to outline the course, what readings to assign, how to focus lectures, and so on. Persons for whom these decisions are an essential component of the teaching process will probably not be suited to teaching via television. On the other hand, by being freed from time-consuming tasks and details, the teacher can concentrate on the presentation of the material, which takes on added importance in reaching the long-distance learner.

This emphasis on presentation suggests an obvious pitfall: the temptation for teachers of adults and those who engage their services to place performance values ahead of substantive educational goals. If, as the pro-technologists predict, the teacher of tomorrow addressing vast audiences via telecommunication will be a star in the educational firmament, does it follow that an attractive personality and style of delivery will supersede hard-won knowledge and a serious commitment to teaching?

A few institutions have worked out a compromise between the television screen and the classroom. In addition to viewing the programs, students electing to take the telecourses for credit must attend an orientation session plus three discussion meetings, pass one or more exams, and submit a final paper that reflects their individual interests. In this system, the teacher acts as a mentor, available to guide and counsel the student throughout the course.

Generally, the technique that works best in teaching by television is the lecture-discussion (with interactive feature) supplemented by visual aids or demonstrations. Panel programs can also be effective if the panelists are good communicators and the moderator is skillful. To be avoided at all costs is the straight lecture or "talking head" technique.

Quality Control

The concern with quality is a particularly thorny issue. "I cannot stress too vigorously nor too often," says D. B. Varner, former president of the University of Mid-America, "my concern about the quality of the course materials we produce and offer to the public. . . . Monitoring quality . . . has been the historical role of faculties on the campuses, and we are now working, for the most part, without the benefit of this thoughtful, deliberate mechanism of insuring quality."[10] But advocates of open learning maintain that, even without this form of quality control, the British Open University has consistently offered high-quality education that has been given high marks by the academic community.

The Basic Connection

Putting aside the crystal ball and taking a historical view, it appears that, so far, the advance of technology has not significantly altered the basic connection between teacher and learner joined in the common purpose of acquiring knowledge and understanding. From the one-room schoolhouse in the country village to the open university serving a national audience with the aid of sophisticated technology, the teaching-learning process at its best has always involved dedicated teachers and motivated learners. It seems reasonable to assume that this process will continue as in the past, with or without telecommunications.

As a teacher of adults, you are on the cutting edge of change. Whatever the future may hold, it is your teaching skills and dedication that will help bring about the personal and social change for the better that is the ultimate goal and reward of all adult education.

REFERENCES

1. Alan D. Entine, "The Role of Continuing Education," *Women in Midlife—Security and Fulfillment,* U.S. Government Printing Office, Washington, D.C., 1978, part I.
2. Eugene Kennedy, "The Looming Eighties,' *New York Times Magazine,* December 2, 1979.
3. Joe Coates, "Population and Education: How Demographic Trends Will Shape the U.S.," *The Futurist,* February 1978.
4. Quoted in Coates, ibid.
5. Dan Hulbert, "What the Future Will Look Like," *New York Times,* April 20, 1980.

6. Robert McCabe, *Future Directions for Open Learning,* The National Institute of Education, December 1979, Washington, D.C., p. 44.
7. National Institute of Education, op. cit., passim.
8. Martin Greenberger, ed., *Computers, Communications and the Public Interest,* The Johns Hopkins Press, Baltimore, Md., 1971.
9. James Martin, *The Wired Society,* Prentice-Hall, Englewood Cliffs, N.J., 1979.
10 Ronald Gross, National Institute of Education, op. cit., p. 15.

BIBLIOGRAPHY

BOOKS

Issues, Problems

Apps, Jerold W. *Problems in Continuing Education.* New York: McGraw-Hill, 1979.
Freier, Paulo. *Education for A Critical Consciousness.* New York: Seabury Press, 1973.
Gross, Ronald. *The Lifelong Learner.* New York: Simon and Schuster, 1977.
Knowles, Malcolm. *The Adult Learner: A Neglected Species.* Houston: Gulf Publishing
Co., 1973.
————. *The Modern Practice of Adult Education: Andragogy Versus Pedagogy.* New York:
Association Press, 1970.
Postman, N., and C. Weingartner. *Teaching as a Subversive Activity.* New York: Delta
Books, 1969.

Techniques, Strategies, Study Skills

Apps, Jerold W. *Study Skills: For Those Adults Returning to School.* New York: McGraw-
Hill, 1978.
Bergevin, Paul, Dwight Morris, and Robert M. Smith. *Adult Education Procedures.* New
York: Seabury Press, 1963.
Dale, Edgar. *Building A Learning Environment.* Bloomington, Ind.: Phi Beta Kappa,
1972.
Eble, Kenneth. *The Craft of Teaching.* San Francisco: Jossey-Bass, 1976.
Kidd, J. R. *How Adults Learn.* rev. ed. New York: Association Press, 1973.
Knowles, Malcolm. *Self-Directed Learning.* New York: Association Press, 1975.
Mager, R. F. *Preparing Instructional Objectives.* Palo Alto, Calif.: Fearon Publishing,
1962.
Snyder, Robert E., and Curtis Ulmer. *Guide to Teaching Techniques for Adult Classes.*
Englewood Cliffs, N.J.: Prentice-Hall, 1972.

Adult Development

Bühler, Charlotte. *Psychology for Contemporary Living,* New York: Hawthorne Books,
1968.

Erikson, Erik. *Childhood and Society.* New York: Norton, 1963.

Gould, Roger. *Transformations.* New York: Simon and Schuster, 1978.

Knox, Alan B. *Adult Development and Learning.* San Francisco: Jossey-Bass, 1981.

Levinson, Daniel J. *The Seasons of A Man's Life.* New York: Ballantine Books, 1978.

McLeish, John A. B. *The Ulyssean Adult: Creativity in the Middle and Later Years.* Scarborough, Ont.: McGraw-Hill Ryerson Limited 1976.

Open Learning, Technology

Greenberger, Martin, ed. *Computers, Communications and the Public Interest.* Baltimore: The Johns Hopkins University Press, 1971.

Martin, James *The Wired Society.* Englewood Cliffs, N.J.: Prentice-Hall, 1979.

Semple, Robert B., Jr. "New British Export: The Open University." *New York Times,* November 16, 1975.

Psychology

Maslow, Abraham H. *Toward a Psychology of Being.* Princeton, N.J.: Van Nostrand, 1968.

Miller, Jean Baker. *Toward a New Psychology of Women.* Boston: Beacon Press, 1976.

Rogers, Carl. *On Becoming a Person.* Boston: Houghton Mifflin, 1961.

Special Groups

Forbes, Jack D. *Education of the Culturally Different: A Multicultural Approach.* Berkeley, Calif.: Far West Laboratory for Educational Research and Development, 1969.

Houle, Cyril O. *Continuing Education for the Professionals.* San Francisco: Jossey-Bass, 1980.

Lindo, Benice. *Black Ghetto Dialect.* Los Angeles: Instant Phonics, 1972.

General

Cross, Patricia K. *Adult Learners.* San Francisco Jossey-Bass, 1981.

Epstein, Joseph, Ed. *Masters: Portraits of Great Teachers,* New York, Basic Books, 1981.

JOURNALS OF INTEREST TO TEACHERS OF ADULTS

Adult Education: A Journal of Research and Theory, The Otis Bldg., 810 18th St., N.W., Washington, D.C. 20036

Canadian Journal of University Continuing Education, Johnston Hall, University of Guelph, Guelph, Ontario, Canada

Change Magazine, NBW Tower, New Rochelle N.Y. 10801

The Chronicle of Higher Education, 1333 New Hampshire Avenue, Washington, D.C. 20036

Continuum, National University Extension Association, One Dupont Circle, Washington, D.C. 20036

Lifelong Learning: The Adult Years, Adult Education Association of the United States, The Otis Bldg., 810 18th St., N.W., Washington, D.C. 20036

REPORTS

Clearinghouse in Career Education — Adult Learning: Issues and Innovations, ed. by Robert M. Smith, July 1976

National Institute of Education — Future Directions for Open Learning, A Report Based on an Invitational Conference on Open Learning, ed. by Ronald Gross, Dec. 1979

National Institute of Education — Conference Report: Adult Learning Needs and The Demand for Lifelong Learning, ed. by Charles B. Stalford, November 1978

U.S. Department of Health, Education and Welfare — Lifelong Learning and Public Policy, A Report Prepared by the Lifelong Learning Project, February 1978

Educational Policy Research Center — The Future of Adult Education and Learning in the United States, Report prepared for Division of Adult Education, USOE, February 1977

Ontario Institute for Studies in Education — Major Learning Efforts: Recent Research and Future Directions, Allen Tough, 1977

UNESCO — Recommendations on the Development of Adult Education, 19th Session, Nairobi, 1976

Select Committee on Aging — Women in Midlife—Security and Fulfillment, Part I, U.S. Government Printing Office, 1978

Commission on Nontraditional Study — Diversity by Design, Jossey-Bass Publishers, San Francisco, 1975

RESOURCES

GUEST SPEAKERS

Part-time teachers who have full-time occupations outside of teaching often rely on colleagues to serve as guest speakers; however, speakers with a specific kind of expertise can be recruited from community organizations such as the chamber of commerce, League of Women Voters, the American Association of University Women, the parent-teacher association, consumer and conservation groups, minority groups, trade unions, business and industrial corporations, and professional associations. Public officials (when not running for office) are usually available for speaking engagements, as are authors who are in the locality on book promotion tours.

LEARNING RESOURCES

Audiovisual materials are available from many sources aside from commercial rental firms, whose fees often exceed the average budget for an adult education class or program. Films, videotapes, and audiotapes can be obtained either without charge or for modest fees from schools, libraries, civic and community groups, business and industrial corporations, and professional associations. Some trade associations provide films, upon request, that have excellent educational value; for example, the Association of American Railroads has several fine films on the history of railroads in the United States; the American Bar Association has a selection of films for educational purposes—among them *In Search of Justice,* a series on the judicial system in the United States. Materials on aging can be had from the Institute of Gerontology, The University of Michigan-Wayne State University and the Ethel Andrus Gerontology Center at the University of Southern California. An assortment of materials on women's issues and activities is obtainable from women's resource centers in colleges and universities; a multimedia kit about women including records, slides, articles, photos, stories, poems is offered by the Ontario Institute for Studies in Education in Toronto. Many of the state art councils and humanities committees, funded by the National Endowments of the Arts and Humanities, have supported multimedia projects that have produced audiovisual and print materials sometimes available for educational use.

Appendix A

NONCREDIT ADULT EDUCATION REGISTRATION BY FIELD AND LEVEL

Registrations in Noncredit Adult and Continuing Education Activities in Colleges and Universities by Field of Instruction and Level of Institution, U.S., 1978

SUBJECT AREA	REGISTRATIONS (THOUSANDS)			
	TOTAL	UNIVER- SITIES	OTHER 4-YEAR	2-YEAR
Total	10,154	2,691	2,230	5,233
Agriculture and natural resources	234	157	21	56
Business and management	1,070	419	295	356
Education	556	195	200	161
Engineering	247	147	47	53
Fine and applied arts	968	220	206	542
Foreign languages	135	19	23	93
Health professions	1,245	333	454	458
Home economics	720	56	45	619
Law	121	70	22	29
Letters	114	32	31	51
Psychology	193	46	47	100
Public affairs and services	318	135	71	112
Social scientes	246	128	64	54
Theology	184	97	57	30
Interdisciplinary studies	698	239	166	293
Developmental activities	597	22	59	516
Physical education and avocational instruction	800	81	98	621
Other academic areas	422	165	97	160

Business technologies	322	36	46	240
Health technologies	321	13	84	224
Engineering and mechanical technologies	309	30	16	263
Public service technologies	232	39	74	119
Other technologies	102	12	7	83

Source: The national estimates reported in this study were based upon a sample of 484 colleges and universities. A detailed report will be available later. For additional information or to be notified when the report is available, contact Robert Calvert, Jr., National Center for Education Statistics, Room 3071, 400 Maryland Ave., SW, Washington, D.C. 20202 (202/245–8340).

Appendix B

U.S. POPULATION AGED 45 to 64 FROM 1900 to 2050

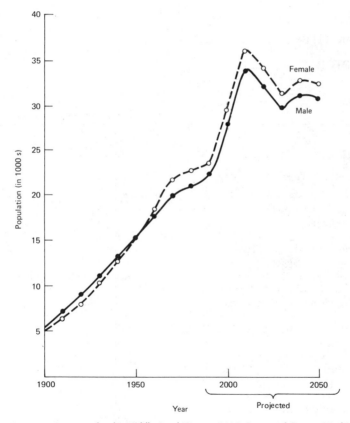

Adapted from Figure 1, "Prospects for the Middle Aged Woman," U.S. Bureau of Census, Washington, D.C., p. 333.

Appendix C

PROGRAM AND INSTRUCTOR EVALUATION

PROGRAM TITLE _____

INSTRUCTOR _____

DATE _____

		(Please check one)		
	EXCELLENT	ABOVE AVERAGE	FAIR	DULL
1. Instructor's Teaching Ability				
2. Instructor's Knowledge of the Subject				
3. Instructor's Attitude Toward Subject				
4. Instructor's Encouraging Discussion & Asking Questions				
5. Instructor's Attitude Toward Participants				
6. Instructor's Ability to Communicate				
7. Practicality of Information Presented				
8. Organization of Program				

9. Material Clearly Presented to Audience				
10. Use of Audiovisual Aids				

11. What part of the program did you find *most beneficial*?
12. What part of the program did you find *least beneficial*?
13. Were facilities, location, parking, dining, lighting, and seating satisfactory?

   Yes _____ No _____. If no, please comment.
14. What day of the week is best for you for this program? Please circle one:

   Mon.   Tue.   Wed.   Thur.   Fri.   Sat.   Sun.

15. How did you learn about this program? Please check:
   ☐ [Institution] Catalogue   ☐ TV Ad
   ☐ Special Brochure   ☐ Radio
   ☐ Ad in Local Newspaper   ☐ Friend
   ☐ *Wall Street Journal* Ad   ☐ Other
16. Did the course measure up to the catalogue description? Yes _____ No _____
   (If no, please explain).
17. What other programs, seminars, workshops, conference topics would you like to see offered by [Institution] to assist you in your personal and professional growth?
18. Additional comments: Please use reverse side of page if necessary.

   When completed, please turn in to the instructor or the monitor.
   Thank you.

Appendix D

SAMPLE EVALUATION FORM

1. What was your principal purpose in taking this course?
   (a) Improving job-related skills
   (b) In-service credit
   (c) Credential requirement
   (d) Credit toward a college degree
   (e) Certification by the state or a professional society
   (f) Credit toward an extension certificate
   (g) Personal development
   (h) Enjoyment/general interest
2. Extent to which this purpose was being fulfilled?
3. Extent to which your overall expectations were being fulfilled?
4. To what extent were program goals and objectives clearly identified?
5. To what extent was the material that was presented congruent with program objectives?
6. To what extent were the course content and organization congruent with your expectations?
7. To what extent was the material presented well organized?
8. To what extent were presentations and activities well planned and organized?
9. To what extent were presentations and explanations clear and understandable?
10. To what extent did the instructor demonstrate a thorough, accurate, and up-to-date knowledge of the subject matter?
11. To what extent was the level of instruction geared to your level of understanding?
12. To what extent was the pace of instruction geared to your learning needs?
13. To what extent did the instructor provide opportunities for discussion and participative activities?
14. To what extent was the instructor responsive to student needs and interests?
14a. To what extent was the classroom environment conducive to independent thinking?
15. To what extent did the instructor hold your interest?
16. To what extent did the instructor speak audibly, clearly, and colorfully?
17. To what extent did the course materials (textbook, handouts, references, films) assist your learning?

18. To what extent was the instructor respectful and impartial in relationships with students?
19. To what extent was the instructor approachable for consultation and assistance?
20. To what extent was the instructor effective in helping you to fulfill your learning needs?
21. To what extent were assignments reasonable and clearly explained?
22. To what extent were assignments/projects/tests congruent with course objectives and material covered?
22a. To what extent were tests/projects/or other assessment procedures well designed to measure achievement of course objectives?
23. To what extent were tests, papers, or projects promptly reviewed and returned?
24. To what extent was the quality of feedback in reviewing, exams, papers, and projects helpful to you?
25. To what extent were grading standards and procedures clearly explained early in the course?
26. To what extent was grading fair in relation to the standards (stated or implied)?

Your reasons for withdrawing:
There were other demands on my time.
The course was too difficult.
The course required too much time and effort.
I lost interest in the subject.
I was dissatisfied with the instructor.
I was dissatisfied with the course content.

Please explain further _____

_____

_____

_____

_____

_____

_____

_____

_____

INDEX